A Difficult Decision

A Compassionate Book About Abortion

by Joy Gardner

Revised Second Edition

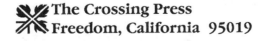
The Crossing Press
Freedom, California 95019

NOTE TO THE READER

The remedies described herein are given as information, and not as a prescription. Although based upon information gathered from the personal experience of a number of individuals, these remedies have neither been tested on a broad sample of individuals, nor scientifically established. Therefore, neither the author nor the publisher can take responsibility for any ill effects which may be produced as a result of using these remedies: the reader does so at his or her own risk.

Copyright © 1986 by Joy Gardner
Cover design, illustration, and text design by Betsy Bayley
Typeset by Giles Bayley
Printed in the U.S.A. by McNaughton & Gunn of Ann Arbor, Michigan

Library of Congress Cataloging-in-Publication Data

Gardner, Joy.
   A difficult decision.

   Bibliography: p.
   1. Abortion. I. Title.
RG734.G37 1986   618.8'8   86-16201
ISBN 0-89594-215-1
ISBN 0-89594-214-3 (pbk.)

Table of Contents

Preface

The purpose of this book is to give support to the woman (or couple*) who finds herself unexpectedly pregnant. For most women, this is a profound crisis.

If you are pregnant, and if you feel ambivalent about having an abortion, I want to encourage you to explore your options carefully. Too often there are social pressures, family pressures, and peer pressures which make a clear decision difficult.

I believe that a woman should be free to make her own choice, because carrying a baby for nine months and/or raising a child is a profound commitment.

I believe that women who definitely do not want a baby should be given abortions. Our society does not allow a man to use a woman's body without her consent—how then can we consider forcing a woman to carry a child to term within her body, when she does not want that child? Recent studies clearly indicate that the mother's emotional well-being (or lack of it) during pregnancy has a profound effect upon the baby. And I have found in my practice that adopted children often suffer from feelings of unworthiness and chronic fear of abandonment. And parents who have children that they do not want are most likely to be abusive toward those children. Compulsory pregnancy simply does not make sense. Children are such a blessing—when they are truly wanted. I believe we should have fewer children, and take better care of the ones we have.

---

*I address this book primarily to women because so many women are alone during this time. But I know that men can be deeply involved in this experience. Please understand that I am talking to you also—the men who care.

I find that many women *want* to keep their babies, *but lack the resources to do so.* I believe that far more abortions could be prevented if people would stop trying to force women to have babies that they don't want, and turn their attention to the women who want to have babies but lack the resources.

On the other hand, many women feel pressured to have abortions which they later regret. Please be extremely careful; unwanted abortions can traumatize your body, mind, and spirit.

"What do I *really want?*" is the question that I encourage you to ask yourself. If you follow your own deepest sense of what is right for you (as an individual or a couple), then you will come to a decision that you can live with, even if other people call it irrational, immoral, or impractical.

I believe that early tests for pregnancy should be widely available. With these tests, women can find out if they are pregnant within 7-10 days after conception. Once they have this information, they can seek counseling if they wish, and pursue the choice which is most appropriate for them.

If women choose to have abortions, I think they should have ready access to an early vacuum abortion, which can be done up to 8 weeks after the last menstrual period. This can be done in a doctor's office or a clinic in about 10 minutes.

Many women are forced to jump needless hurdles before they can "qualify" for an abortion that they clearly want or need. The possible emotional and physical damage increases with every week of waiting. Late abortions can be devastating not just for the woman and her partner, but also for the doctors and nurses and anyone who participates in them.

I believe in providing the best possible counseling for women and couples who find themselves unexpectedly pregnant. Women who are ambivalent (and *most* women are!) need help in sorting out their feelings and assessing their resources.

Any highly significant decision must come from the the heart, the gut, and the spirit, as well as the mind. For women, particularly, the emotive, intuitive right brain must participate in decision making, along with the rational left brain. This book gives guidelines for involving the whole person in coming to a clear decision before an abortion. These guidelines will be useful for both individuals and counselors.

* * *

I'm a woman and a mother, and I've experienced abortion. I've been trained as a paramedic at a women's clinic, where I assisted with abortions as well as births.

Currently, I'm in private practice as a wholistic practitioner and counselor, specializing in death and loss issues. I've found that many women carry emotional scars from abortions, some of which happened long ago.

In addition to individual death and loss counseling, I teach a two-day experiential workshop called Living with Death and Loss, which is part of my Vibrational Healing series. I conduct these workshops in Santa Cruz, Maui, and elsewhere. Through the use of emotional release, in-depth counseling, stress management, nutrition, herbs, visualization and color therapy, I have helped many women and couples—in groups and individually—to work through their pain and to reach a place of peace. The Death and Loss workshop enables people to work through their personal losses. Many women and men who have been through painful abortions have experienced profound healings during these workshops.

For more information, write to Healing Yourself, P.O. Box 3414, Santa Cruz, California 95063.

Joy Gardner

"If a woman becomes pregnant but does not wish to have the baby, there is indeed a great conflict. Then she must follow her inner guidance and awareness.If she chooses an abortion, there is sorrow, the sorrow as when a blossom melts with the first snow. But existence is accepting of what is."

(Channelled by a woman who cured herself of cervical cancer through visualization and other natural methods)

Getting Oriented

Welcome

Welcome, dear Sister. I'm sorry I don't know you.

I don't know if you're around 40 and afraid this may be your last chance to have a baby.

I don't know if you're single and have always wanted a baby, but your boyfriend doesn't want to settle down.

Or if you're married with four kids and just can't handle another.

Or if you're in the middle of medical school and can't afford to stop right now.

Or if you're only fifteen and are terrified of telling your parents.

Or if you were raped and don't want to bring a child into the world that way.

I don't know if you had an abortion long ago and are still hurting from it.

Whatever your situation, I know it isn't easy for you.

The Decision

Virtually everyone goes through feeling ambivalent about having a baby—even when a pregnancy is planned. And certainly everyone seems to experience some ambivalence when considering an abortion. There's no commitment that can compare with that of becoming a parent. For most people, having a baby means having another person in your life, permanently. This can be the greatest gift in the world—if you're ready for it. But it's not something to take lightly.

For couples, the act of having a baby is far more binding than marriage. As a parent, you cannot get a divorce from your child. And if you and your partner split up, you're much more likely to continue seeing each other because of the child you share. Genetically, the child takes on characteristics of both its parents, so when you look at and live with the child, you will often be reminded of the child's other parent.

Many couples underestimate the profound repercussions that an abortion will have on their relationship. This doesn't mean that an abortion is wrong for them. It does mean that it's a decision to make together, by discussing it thoroughly, and by being sensitive to one another's feelings. (Please see pages 22-23.)

Many women believe they would be incapable of raising a child alone. Yet I have seen single mothers—and some very young mothers—who adored their children and were excellent parents. In fact, a broad survey of hundreds of parents in North America (taken by Dr. Harold A. Minden and reported in his book, *Two Hugs for Survival*—a great book about parenting) showed that 32% of single-parent families found parenting to be fulfilling and positive. That may not sound like a lot, but only 22% of two-parent families found parenting to be fulfilling and positive!

On the other hand, if you aren't ready for it, think twice, whether you have a partner or not, because a whopping 46% of single-parent families and a whopping 41% of two-parent families found parenting to be a frustrating and negative experience.

* * *

One tool that's helpful in decision-making is to take a sheet of paper and make two columns. In the first column, write down everything in favor of having a baby. In the second column, write down everything opposed to it. This allows you to take all the thoughts and feelings that go round and round in your head and put them out where you can get a good look at them.

This is an opportunity to assess your situation realistically. Do you have supportive relatives, close friends who would like to help with the baby? What are your financial resources? Have you received unbiased, professional counseling, and if so, what insights has this given you? Are there support groups in your area which you could turn to (a group for unwed mothers, a single-parents group)? Do you feel that you're emotionally stable and reasonably mature? Do you like children?

In the final analysis, becoming a parent is usually not a rational choice. When you think about all the time, energy and money that go into raising one child, hardly any people in their right mind would choose to take on such a project! But the desire to love and nurture another human being does not come from the head. So pay attention to your gut feelings. Please see the visualizations described on pages 44 through 47. And then I'd suggest that you let the choice come from your heart— which combines the mind and the emotions.

Take the time you need to make a good decision and remember that you can change your mind at almost any point. But take the necessary precautions by making an appointment with your doctor immediately, as a back-up, in case you do decide to have an abortion.

Finally, remember that whatever decision you make will be the best decision that you are capable of making—given the inner and outer resources available to you. Please, be gentle with yourself.

Who Are We to Judge?

Carol's a housewife with three children, ages 3, 5, and 8. She loves kids and her children are well-adjusted and happy. She became pregnant just before her husband's appointment to get a vasectomy. He works at a lumber mill, and they barely get by. There have been a lot of lay-offs, and he fears for his job. Carol's mother lives with them—she requires a great deal of attention. Their decision to have an abortion was a painful one, but they felt it would be irresponsible to bring a fourth child into the world when their own future is so uncertain.

Ron and Betty live under similar circumstances. They have three small children. She unexpectedly became pregnant. His job is also unstable. But this couple did not believe in abortion so they elected to have the baby, whom they now cherish even though the stress on Betty and on the other children is often severe.

Who is to say which of these couples made the right choice? Each made the choice which felt most deeply right to them.

Elaine is emotionally and financially impoverished. She doesn't want a child. She deeply resents being pregnant. She hates the man who made her pregnant. She hates the world that expects her to care for a child she doesn't want. What are her choices? If she has the child, she could hate it for ruining her life. The child could suffer from neglect and child abuse. Elaine already uses alcohol and drugs. If Elaine should give the child up for adoption, she'd feel so guilty that she'd hate herself. And there is strong evidence that the child would carry the scars of Elaine's hatred all through life. Elaine chose to have an abortion.

Ananda is only 18. Her boyfriend already has a daughter by a previous marriage and he threatens to leave if she has this baby. But Ananda has been through an abortion just six months ago, and she can't do it again. In her dreams she sees herself playing with a happy little girl. Her parents want her to have an abortion. Her friends assume that she will. But she feels strong and confident. She makes the decision to keep her baby. She knows it is the right choice.

Ron and Beverly have been outspoken in condemning abortion

until they found themselves unexpectedly pregnant, with four kids to support, the youngest only eight months old. With great aversion, they decide to have an abortion.

Who are we to judge?

Support for Keeping the Baby

It's sad to have an abortion and later find yourself wishing that you had kept the baby. Being a mother (or father) is one of the most wonderful things that can happen to you, so it's worth fighting for. I'd suggest that you start out by getting the best counseling you can find. Go to Planned Parenthood. There are many women's organizations with trained abortion counselors. Find friends you can confide in. Don't rush into an abortion. Think it out thoroughly. But while you're thinking, do make an appointment with your doctor as a back-up.

Meanwhile, don't be shy about asking your mother and other members of your family and your friends if they'd be willing to help. Sometimes the results are surprising. There may be people who would like to get involved. I know several second parents or godparents or honorary aunts and uncles. They're often people who've chosen not to have children of their own and are delighted to have an ongoing relationship with someone else's child. Big Brother is a thriving organization built on this principle. But the deepest bond is made just after the baby is born, so if you know someone who wants to get involved, try to have those persons with you at the birth, or very soon thereafter.

If you're considering keeping the baby, your major fear may be that you won't have enough money to support a child. I hope that someday the so-called Pro Life movement will focus on giving more practical help to women who want to keep their babies. At present, they are preoccupied with lobbying for legislation which would make abortions illegal. Their singleminded support of the unborn makes them unwilling to consider the woman's needs. The Pro Life philosophy is by definition anti choice, whereas the Pro Choice position is that a woman should be free to make her own choice, and she should be supported in her decision, whether it is to keep the child or to have an abortion.

If you're reasonably certain that you want to keep the child, you could turn to organizations like Birthright (which is Pro Life in philosophy) or Crisis Pregnancy Center (which is Christian in approach).

They sometimes offer financial assistance and will help establish contacts with professional counselors, lawyers and doctors. They may help cover medical costs, give referrals to shelter or group homes, and assist in other practical ways. If you are considering adoption, they will help with this. But if you go to such an organization, you may want to take a friend with you for support. Feel free to leave if you aren't getting the kind of help you want. If you're a teenager and you want to keep the child, be wary of groups that may pressure you to give up the child for adoption rather than helping you to support the child yourself. You might start by going to a women's clinic or women's center, and ask them to refer you to the group(s) in your area which would best meet your needs. Another option for a pregnant woman is to place your child with temporary foster parents.

For women who are looking for ways to support themselves while keeping their babies, Sharon F. Smith in *Mothering Magazine* calls upon the "great courage, strength, flexibility and creativity of the human spirit of a mother who wants to be with her baby." She makes the following suggestions: a mother and family can share their house to keep expenses down. If she shares with another woman who has a child, they can get together on child care. Or she can rent a room to someone who is willing to help out with the child, in exchange for cheaper rent. A mother can work at home—providing day care, grading papers for local teachers, tutoring, typing and editing, or doing bookkeeping. She can take care of an elderly or handicapped person, or provide a foster home for a special needs child. Or she can come up with a totally innovative idea, like the woman who opened up a toy rental business in her basement. There are also some jobs where you can take your child with you, like the letter carrier in a rural area who takes her child on deliveries.

Then there are cooperative babysitting arrangements as the baby gets a little older. One neighborhood co-op has 5 families with children ranging from 1–4 years old. Each family starts with 10 tickets, representing hours of babysitting they can trade amongst themselves. For more information, please read *The Heart Has Its Own Reasons* by Mary Ann Cahill (available from La Leche League).

Support for Having an Abortion

If you decide to have an abortion, you're going to need a support system. You need friends you can talk to. Be careful about whom you open up to, but try to find an empathetic friend. Many areas have Women's Clinics or Women's Support Groups, and these are usually safe places to find a sympathetic ear. If possible, it's also helpful to attend a counseling session or a workshop with someone trained in facilitating emotional release. In fact, if you fail to do these things, you may find yourself carrying the effects of this abortion for a long time. And it will probably come up again if you decide to have a baby in the future.

It is never to late to work it through. Even if your abortion happened 20 or 40 years ago, it is still possible to re-live those events and bring yourself to a point of acceptance. (Please see pages 44-46.)

When you go for an abortion, try to arrange to have someone take you there and pick you up. It's important to have the physical support and it's comforting to have someone to talk to. It also helps to have someone to hold you.

If it can be arranged, it can be comforting to have your partner or a friend with you during an early abortion, to hold your hand and to remind you to breathe deeply (which helps to overcome the pain).

Please leave yourself at least one full day of *rest* after the abortion. Even if it's an early abortion and your feeling fine the next day, it really helps to take the time to integrate this experience into your life, your mind, your feelings, and your body.

Adoption

When a woman gives her child up for adoption, it is often done out of love, out of a sincere belief that the adoptive parents will be able to offer this child the security and material comforts that she cannot provide. And when the adoptive parents take a baby into their homes and hearts, it is almost always with the best of intentions.

I know families whose adopted children are well-loved and grow up as very productive and happy people. But it would be misleading if I did not describe my own experience and that of other counselors in working with people who have been adopted. If you are considering adoption, consider this information, but consider it with a grain of salt. Adoption practices are changing very rapidly, and the difficulties that adoptees have experienced in the past will probably be mitigated by these changing policies.

Twenty years ago, when a woman gave her baby up for adoption, it was a way of wiping the slate clean, and she believed that that was the end of it. But now we find that many adopted children desperately want to know who their birth parents are. And many mothers never forget their babies and long to be able to meet them. An organization called Parents Finders in Canada, and Orphan Voyage in the United States (Cedaredge, Colorado 81413) enables adopted children and their birth parents to file their names if they desire to find one another.

I've heard wonderful stories about tearful reunions, particularly between birth mothers and their daughters. But I've also heard sad stories of children who longed to meet their birth parents but were consistently refused. "That's a part of my past and I want to forget it," some mothers replied. And then there are mothers who want so much to meet their children, but their children never show an interest.

Most adopted children want to know *why* they were given up for adoption. They want to know if their mothers cared about them. No matter how soon after birth they were adopted, and no matter how kind their adoptive parents were, they are often plagued by a sense of unworthiness. As infants or children, they interpret the abandonment as a sign of their own shortcomings. (If they aren't told about being adopted until they are older, they often see it as a betrayal and deception.)

In my counseling practice, I've found that these are the clients who suffer from a chronic feeling of insecurity: every time someone they love leaves or threatens to leave, they interpret this as confirmation that they're undeserving, unloved, and unloveable. The feeling of being abandoned is so powerful that they go through periods of being unable to cope with their lives.

Most—not all—of the women I've known who were left by their mothers at an early age feel deeply wounded in their ability to be mothers. Either they do not want to have children of their own, or if they do have children, they feel as if something is missing—they can't connect with their children on a deep heart level. I believe this is because they identify with their original mother, and since they were not mothered by her, they feel inadequate to provide mothering for their own children.

The effect that adoption has on the mothers is also quite painful. The women I've seen who carried their babies to term and then gave them up, suffer far more from feelings of guilt than those who chose to have abortions. Yet so many women chose to give up their babies *because* they care about them, and because they're convinced that someone else can provide a better home than they can. There are certainly adopted children and birth mothers who do not carry such deep scars. I'm confident that there are circumstances when this *is* the right decision. Each case is unique and must be considered on its own terms. If you are considering an adoption, please seek the help of an unbiased counselor who can assist you in exploring your feelings and options. As one adoptee pointed out, "Given the choice of whether to live or not—regardless of what challenges I've had to meet—I'd prefer to be alive."

There are alternatives now available to women who want to give up their babies for adoption. There are open adoption agencies such as Golden Cradle in suburban Philadelphia which offer an adoption policy in which the birth mother receives letters from various couples who want to adopt a child. Then *she chooses* the parents whom she wants for her baby, and after the baby is born she personally gives the baby to its new parents. Mothers who choose this agency say that seeing the joy on the faces of the new parents makes them feel much better about giving up the baby. And later, the child can choose whether or not to meet his/her birth mother. For more information, you can write to Community and Family Services, 1000 Hastings, Traverse City, Michigan 49684 or Catholic Charities, P.O. Box 1931, Jacksonville, Florida 32201, or Lutheran Social Services, 19230 Forest Park Drive, NE Seattle, Washington 98155 and Lutheran Social Services of Texas, 615 Elm St., San Antonio, Texas 78202.

Please see page 100 for an adoption story which opens yet another possibility.

For Men

Dear Brother, I don't know if this is a baby that you would love and cherish. Or if it's a totally unwanted event. Or if you feel particularly uninvolved and unemotional. Or if you're feeling angry or guilty.

Sometimes an abortion is very difficult for a man. Maybe you want to have a child but haven't the time for one, or couldn't support one, or perhaps your partner isn't ready. Maybe you don't want a child and you feel victimized by the pregnancy. Perhaps your partner allowed you to think it was a "safe" time, and then held you responsible for it. Or maybe you feel guilty for not taking the initiative to make sure birth control was used. Or perhaps this is the first time you've made a woman pregnant and there's a feeling of pride in knowing that you can father a baby. You may find it difficult to sort out your feelings and decide what *you* want—particularly at a time when everyone seems to expect you to be strong and supportive. But your feelings are important. If you can give yourself permission to *express* your emotions and explore your own needs in this situation, it will help you to feel better. (Please read pages 89-90 on Releasing Emotions.)

Whatever you feel, there is usually a grieving process which occurs around an abortion, and one of the stages of grieving is anger. So if you feel that anger is coming up, it helps to find a safe way of discharging it. It's helpful to talk about whatever may be disturbing you. You may find your anger turning to tears. Or you may simply need to cry rather than get angry. Men usually aren't encouraged to cry, but I'd like to encourage you. Your grief is natural, and you have every reason to feel sad. If you share your feelings with your partner (if you care to be close to her), it can deepen your relationship. Don't be afraid to express your emotions. Most women feel closer to men who are able to cry; it gives them permission to be more open about their own feelings. And tears that are shed often help release us from the clutches of sorrow, and clear the way for acceptance. (Please read pages 84-86 on Grieving.)

An abortion is an extremely traumatic time for most couples. It's always unexpected, inconvenient, and tends to be highly emotional. Since the hormones of pregnancy are already at work during this most sensitive early part of pregnancy, many women experience morning sickness, weakness, nausea, irritability, and a desire to be taken care of—just when they have to be making a painful decision which is likely to affect the rest of their lives. The feeling of being emotionally vulnerable and unusually sensitive often lingers for a month or more after the abortion.

The whole experience may have even longer lasting effects on both of you. You and/or your partner may find your whole attitude toward sex changing. In some cases it may deepen your respect for the sexual act. In other cases it may make it difficult to have sex at all. These effects may be short-lived, or they may last indefinitely.

The greatest trauma comes when the woman is in deep conflict over whether or not to have an abortion. Or when there is a conflict between what she wants and what you want. If both of you are in agreement that an abortion is the appropriate decision at this time, it is much more likely to be a relatively pain-free experience and may actually bring you closer together.

I know a man who wanted a child, but then became the lover of a woman who had two children and didn't want more. She unexpectedly became pregnant. The pregnancy ended in an abortion. When this happened two times, he found himself unable to make love to her.

I know a couple who wanted a child, but she became pregnant while he was still in college. They decided it would be better to have an abortion and wait until later. The experience was very painful to her, but he expressed no emotion. She thought he was cold and unfeeling, and after a few months she found she couldn't relate to him and left. About six months later he finally began to get in touch with his own sadness and tried to communicate with her, but it was too late.

If you and your partner can be sympathetic and supportive to each other; if you can express your own feelings openly; if you can support her through possible mood changes, it will help both of you to get through this time without doing harm to each other. It may even be an opportunity to grow closer.

If you talk openly about your fears and desires—about why it might be good to have a child, and why it wouldn't—this will make it much easier to come to a clear decision. You might find yourself considering making some big changes in your life. Though a child might not be convenient now, it could turn out to be easier than having to deal with all the possible repercussions of an abortion. I know many couples who didn't consider marriage until the woman became pregnant. The pregnancy forced them to take their relationship seriously. They decided to get married, making a deeper commitment, and it strengthened their relationship. Think it through carefully. Just how important are your other commitments? As one man put it "Being a father is one of the greatest things that ever happened to me."

If your partner is going to have an abortion, she may want you to be there. Most women have to undergo the trauma of abortion alone, in the presence of strangers. But some doctors will allow the man to be present. This can be very helpful to the woman. The same breathing exercises, eye contact, and hand-holding that ease the pain of childbirth can be extremely important to a woman undergoing an abortion without general anesthetic.

But even if this option is not open to you (or if you find that you just can't do it or if it's not something that seems desirable), most women will welcome your presence immediately before and after an abortion. They will also welcome your understanding sympathy and arms to cry in. You, too, may need the same from her.

Practical Considerations

Calendar

It's often confusing to try to calculate the various dates that are given in relation to your last menstrual period, etc. By writing in the following dates, these calculations should be easier for you. The terms used below will be explained on the following pages.

LMP—Last menstrual period
(the date of the first day of
your last period)   _____

Probable date of conception:
(This is usually, not always, 2
weeks after your LMP—some
women are quite certain when
they conceived.)   _____

Due date of missed period
(If your periods are regular,
you'll know when your next
one is or was due.   _____

THE FOLLOWING MAY NOW BE CALCULATED—

Home Pregnancy Tests and H.C.G. Tests are most reliable 45 days (6 weeks and 3 days) LMP (i.e., 45 days after the first day of your last actual period).

Menstrual Extractions must be done within 6 weeks LMP.

Suction Abortion can be done 6-12 weeks LMP.

Dilation and Evacuation (D&E) can be performed from 14-24 weeks LMP, though it is often done only under 18 weeks.

Abortion by Intrauterine Injection (saline or prosta-glandin) can be used 16-24 weeks LMP, though it is often done only under 20 weeks.

Stages of Development

2 WEEKS LMP—in most cases, fertilization occurs at 2 weeks after the last menstrual period (LMP), while the ovum is travelling down the fallopian tube.

3 WEEKS LMP—a fertilized egg, a human seed, has multiplied into many cells and has reached the uterus where it has implanted in the uterine lining, to obtain nourishment. (It is believed that IUD's work by irritating the uterine lining so that implantation cannot occur.)

4 WEEKS LMP—by the time the next period is due (the one that will be or has been missed), an embryo has begun to form, with a sort of head and tail and arm and leg buds and a yolk sac. At this stage, it resembles a fish embryo. It measures 0.3 inches and there is a rudimentary heart that beats.

5 WEEKS LMP—the face, trunk, and extremities are growing. The brain begins to develop and an umbilical cord starts to form. There are five faint but still connected fingers. The eardrum develops. The embryo measures 0.45 inches.

6 WEEKS LMP—the embryo is about the size of a pea.

8 WEEKS LMP—the embryo is about the size of a thumbnail.It has a heart and liver and 2 sides of the brain can be distinguished. The spinal cord begins to develop.

10 WEEKS LMP—the embryo becomes a fetus, which has begun to assume distinctly human shape. Its muscles move. Eyelids begin to form. The skeleton develops. The fetus measures about 1.6 inches; it is about the size of a plum.

11 WEEKS LMP—the sex organs begin to form. Before this time, it is not possible to see whether the fetus is a boy or a girl. The face begins to look human. The fetus measures about 2 inches.

13 WEEKS LMP—the fetus assumes full term proportions. Its eyes are closed. The forehead and nose become distinct. The lips open and close. Its head turns. Nail beds are formed. It is about 2½ inches long and weighs ¾ of an ounce, the weight of an ordinary letter.

14 WEEKS LMP—the fetus is about 3 inches long, surrounded by an amniotic sac.

20 WEEKS LMP—the fetal heartbeat can be detected, and there may be movement.

24-25 WEEKS LMP or earlier—there is a chance that the fetus might live if aborted or delivered.

* * *

It is ironic that those people who oppose abortions are the same ones who try to prevent early abortions. They are eager to show pictures of the fetus in utero, after 10 weeks LMP. But if you look at earlier pictures, you will see that the embryo does not become a fetus and does not take on human characteristics until 10 weeks after the last menstrual period.

If women insist upon it, the majority of abortions can be performed before 10 weeks LMP. I believe that this would prevent a lot of physical and emotional turmoil.

With existing forms of abortion, I caution women to wait until 6 weeks LMP before having an abortion, because while early vacuum abortions can be done before then, they have a failure rate of 22%, because the fetus is so tiny that it's easy to miss. If menstrual extractions are legalized, they would be the safest and most reliable method, because the lining of the uterus (that which normally sheds during menstruation—and from which the embryo obtains nourishment when there is no menstruation) is removed, along with the embryo.

Pregnancy Tests

Planned Parenthood offices can be found in most cities. They usually offer pregnancy testing; if not, they'll tell you where you can go. Doctors, clinics, and hospitals also offer pregnancy testing.

EARLY TESTING

If women are able to obtain results early, this gives them more time to receive counseling, more time to reach a sound decision. There would still be time to obtain an early vacuum abortion, between 6 and 10 weeks from the last menstrual period.

EARLY URINE TEST—The Test Pak can be taken two weeks after conception, i.e., as soon as the period is missed (4 weeks LMP). It takes 4 minutes to receive the results.

BLOOD TEST—This is now available in most large cities in the U.S. The Mono Clonal Antibody test can be taken 4-7 days after conception (3 weeks LMP). The RIA (Radio Immuno Assay) can be taken 14 days after conception (4 weeks LMP) or when the period is one day late. To obtain these tests, you'll probably need a doctor's referral. They're more expensive than the early urine test, and results take about 24 hours to obtain.

COMMON TESTING

HCG TEST—This is a laboratory test which checks a woman's urine for the hormone Human Chorionic Gonadotrophin, which is manufactured by the body during early pregnancy. You must wait 45 days after your last menstrual period. If your periods are on a regular cycle, that would be about 2 weeks after your missed period or 6 weeks LMP. Results are obtained immediately.

HOME PREGNANCY TEST—This is a urine test which is available in drugstores. It can be used 39 days after the first day of your last menstrual period, but medical workers say it's possible to get a false negative unless you wait until the 45th day. In some women, the body does not manufacture sufficient HCG to show up on the test until the 45th day. Results are obtained immediately.

PLEASE NOTE: Once you get a positive pregnancy test, I'd suggest making arrangements *immediately* to see a doctor and to schedule an abortion. Then arrange *immediately* to see a counselor. This will give you time to make a considered decision while giving you the backup of knowing that *if* you decide to have an abortion, the option of having an early abortion will be available to you.

If you feel certain about wanting an abortion, then try to schedule one for about 6 or 7 weeks LMP. If you feel that you need time to make up your mind, then schedule one for 7 or 8 weeks LMP. If that date arrives and you still need more time, you have up to 12-14 weeks LMP before the procedure becomes more complex, traumatic, and dangerous. Try not to wait more than 12 weeks LMP.

Emmenagogues

If your period is late, you may want to consider using an emmenagogue. This is a remedy which will help to bring on a late period. The following emmenagogues will not induce an abortion. But if you are *not* pregnant, they will usually bring on your period.

VITAMIN E—600-800 I.U. per day. This vitamin works by strengthening the endocrine glands. (It should not be used in this quantity if you have high blood pressure or a rheumatic heart condition.)

BLACK COHOSH—Boil 3 cups of water and add 1 Tbsp. black cohosh and simmer for 10 minutes. Drink 3 cups per day. It should work within 1-3 days.

Dealing with Stress

You stand at a pivotal point in your life, trying to make a clear-minded decision while virtually at gunpoint. Any change in your life—especially an unexpected change—causes a stress reaction in your body. When these reactions build up, it leads to distress, which is experienced as exhaustion, depression, and lowered resistance. These reactions become particularly disturbing when you have to make an important decision.

During stress, your body consumes huge amounts of vitamins B and C, so it's important to replace these vitamins immediately. The adrenal glands also consume large amounts of vitamins A and E. The following nutrients will help you to cope with stress:

VITAMIN B COMPLEX (or Compound)—Find a good B Complex tablet that contains 10-50 mg. of each of these:

B-1 (thiamin)	B-3 (niacin or niacinamide)
B 2 (riboflavin)	B-6 (pyridoxine)

and at least 5 mg. of the following:

pantothenic acid	choline
PABA	inositol

If you're under slight stress, you only need about 10 mg. of each of the major B vitamins per day. With moderate stress, 25-50 mg. per day will do. If you're experiencing severe stress (distress), you can take up to 100 mg. When your urine turns bright yellow you'll know that you're taking plenty of B vitamins and that the excess is being excreted in the urine.

VITAMIN C—This is an essential nutrient during times of stress. Natural vitamin C (which is comparatively expensive) is not necessary to alleviate stress; ascorbic acid is adequate. Take 1000-5000 mg. per day.

CALCIUM WITH MAGNESIUM—Use tablets containing a total of about 800 mg. calcium and 400 mg. magnesium per day. The absorption of calcium requires about half as much magnesium. Shaklee makes an excellent product called Calcium Magnesium Plus. (You can find Shaklee distributors in the yellow pages of your phone book under Health Food Stores.)

PEPPERMINT, CATNIP, AND SCULLCAP TEA—Place 1 tsp. of each herb in a pot and add 2 cups of boiling water. Steep 5 minutes and drink freely.

RESCUE REMEDY—This is one of the finest remedies for stress. It comes as a tincture, and 4 drops may be taken under the tongue, or in ¼ cup of water or fruit juice, every 15 minutes, or 4 times a day, as needed. Please see Appendix A, page 112, for an explanation of this remedy, and how to obtain it.

Another Dimension

The Spirit of the "Baby"

It has been my experience—after guiding hundreds of pregnant women through visualizations—that at least 9 out of 10 women can contact the spirits of their potential babies. You might ask: Are these experiences "real"? I don't think it matters. You might argue that the women are just listening to the voice of their own subconscious, that it is just wish fulfillment. I say that these women are making a vital contact with the subconscious aspect of themselves which is an integral part of the total decision-making process. (My own belief is that visualization enables a woman to contact *both* the spirit of the baby *and* her own subconscious. If the person who is guiding her will ask her to contact her "higher self," she will give her subconscious a voice.)

If it is actually possible for a woman to contact the spirit of her potential baby, this suggests that the "baby" already has a spirit. The question may be asked: Is an abortion a murder? I do not believe it is.

Several years ago, a woman contacted me because she was having recurrent dreams about a little girl. The woman suspected that this girl would be her daughter, *if* she were to become pregnant. But she already had a one-year-old daughter, and she and her husband felt it was too soon to have another child.

Through visualization, I helped her to establish contact with this second potential daughter. The girl told her mother how eager she was to be born because of the healing work she wanted to do. The woman considered her spirit-daughter's request, but she was not ready to comply with her wish. A year later she became pregnant, and gave birth to a baby girl.

In this case, the spirit was apparently present long before the baby was conceived. So the existence of a spirit hardly implies that an abortion is a murder.

* * *

Many women tell me (and I experienced this myself) that during pregnancy they had conversations with their babies-to-be. These experiences might have occurred during dreams or while meditating or walking or through visualizations. These women knew what sex their children would be, and many of the children's personal characteristics.

On the other hand, it cannot be denied that occasionally a woman will have a similar experience, and her predictions will prove to be wrong. These psychic messages are not *always* accurate, but they often are.

For example, before my first son was born, we had several conversations. I didn't literally hear his voice with my ears; it was more like hearing someone talk in my dreams. But I was awake, in fact I was walking. Among other things (all of which were accurate), he told me that his head would be distorted. I was dismayed by this message, but he teased me, "Did you think you'd have a perfect baby?" Then he added, "Don't worry—it won't be serious."

After I had been in labor over 30 hours, the doctor took an X-ray and informed me that my pelvis was small in relation to the size of my baby's head, and that he would probably have to do a cesarean. I stubbornly insisted on doing my Lamaze breathing exercises for another 6 hours until my son was finally born vaginally, with forceps. His poor head was strangely misshappen from having to mold itself through my relatively narrow pelvis. Within a day or two his head became perfectly normal.

For those who believe in reincarnation, these concepts are perfectly logical. Eastern religions teach that the soul chooses its parents and the circumstances of its lifetime as a way of working through karma from previous lives. I believe that an abortion is an experience that the spirit of the mother (or parents) and the spirit of the child share together—both for their own reasons. Usually the karmic lesson requires a whole lifetime, but sometimes it can be learned in a few brief weeks or months. Since the spirit world is outside of time and space, spirits can see into the future. So a spirit would not unwittingly become involved with a body that it knew was likely to be aborted.

When does the soul enter the body of the potential baby? I have heard mystics say between 3 months after conception and 3 weeks after birth. Certainly I have—on rare occasions—seen newborn babies who looked as if there was "nobody home." Yet a prominent astrologer says that the spirit enters the body as the medulla oblongata (at the base of the brain) emerges from the womb.

I do not pretend to know the answers to these mysteries. In a sense, the whole argument is moot because by definition you cannot kill a soul—that lives on whether the body lives or dies. But one wonders whether the potential baby's soul experiences an attachment to the body and feels a loss when an abortion occurs.

Again, based on the visualizations which I have been privileged to attend, I have observed that the soul seems to experience less of an attachment to that piece of flesh than to its chosen parent(s) and the sort of life it might imagine leading under those circumstances.

It seems to me that sometimes the abortion itself is the event which that particular soul came to experience. At other times, there seems to be a genuine bargaining process that takes place, and there is an element of a gamble. I believe that in choosing to have an abortion we are depriving that soul of a very special opportunity. And even a very difficult or challenging lifetime is often just what is needed in order for that soul to work out its particular sort of karma. But any bargaining process involves two (or more) individuals, and each entity must watch out for its own interests. So I don't believe that the potential mother should be a martyr to her own needs and desires just because she feels the pull of this other being's needs and desires.

I believe that the most essential element of this experience is that each being has respect for the other. So if you are considering an abortion, and if you're concerned about how this will affect the spirit of the "baby," I believe it's most helpful to consciously direct your attention to that spirit and describe your own situation as best you can. Then try to listen to the spirit, and consider what it has to say. After you have done this, if you decide to have an abortion, say goodbye as lovingly as possible. (The visualization and information on pages 84 through 94 can be helpful.)

Most interesting to me is that these unborn beings (at least the ones I've contacted or heard about) do not regard abortion as murder. For example, one woman came to me for counseling because she was pregnant and felt ambivalent about having the baby. She wanted the child, but her boyfriend had just gone to China and was very noncommittal about the relationship.

Through visualization, I helped this woman to contact the soul of her "baby." She found herself talking to a boy child who told her that there was a special bond between them, and that she would enjoy him so much that she could handle being a single parent. But he also showed her that he was happy where he was, and she should not feel obliged to go through with the pregnancy if she didn't want to.

She chose to keep the child, and although her boyfriend was only an occasional visitor, the baby boy was indeed a great comfort to her.

I've found that these Spirit Children are always very wise and compassionate. They feel a sweet affection for their "parents," and a deep concern for their well-being.

One woman told me a rather unusual story. When she found herself unexpectedly pregnant, she found herself hearing a voice which sounded like a child's voice (she was not accustomed to "hearing voices"). Repeatedly it pleaded: "Please don't go through with this pregnancy. This is a lesson for both of us. We've been too spontaneous. We have to stop doing this."

She was stunned by the implication that a disembodied soul was capable of making a wrong choice and could actually be a partner in the decision to abort.

Another fascinating story is told by Dr. Gladys T. McGarey, a wholistic physician who specializes in home births. In her book, *Born to Live*, Dr. McGarey admits that when it came to abortions, she was "torn between the two warring factions," until one of her patients told her the following story:

"This mother had a four-year-old daughter whom she would take out to lunch occasionally. They were talking about this thing and that, and the child would shift from one subject to another, when Dorothy suddenly said, "Last time when I was four inches long and in your tummy, Daddy wasn't ready to marry you yet, so I went away. But then I came back." Her eyes lost that faraway look, and she was chatting again about four-year-old matters.

"Mother was silent. No one but her husband, the doctor, and she knew this—she *had* become pregnant about two years before she and her husband were ready to get married. When she was four months pregnant, she decided to have an abortion. She was ready to have the child, but her husband-to-be was not.

"When the two of them did get married and were ready to have their first child, the same entity made its appearance. And the little child was saying, in effect, 'I don't hold any resentments towards you for having had the abortion. I understood. I knew why it was done, and that's okay. So here I am again. It was an experience. I learned from it and you learned from it, so now, let's get on with the business of life.' "

I spoke to another couple who told me that the night before she had her abortion, her husband had a dream, and a child came to him and said, "Don't worry. If I don't come now, I'll come later. I'm in no hurry. The loss is only your own." Two years later they had a daughter whom they believe is the same entity.

Whether or not you believe in such experiences, it is undeniable that an unexpected pregnancy is an event which engages you on all levels: physical, emotional, and spiritual. To relate to this experience only on the physical level is a violation of the other aspects of your total being. Visualizations help to tap into the emotional and spiritual aspects of this experience, and it is not necessary for the facts to be absolutely accurate.

Many women and men long to be able to talk to the being who *would be* their child. Listening to this entity (even if it is just your own subconscious mind, as some people suggest) can be a helpful way of sorting out your feelings so that you are able to make a clear decision.

Getting Centered

Becoming unexpectedly pregnant (or anticipating that you may be) is like having the rug pulled out from under you. Suddenly powerful forces you cannot control are shaping your destiny. Your whole life is in turmoil. Whatever plans you had for your future have to be put on hold.

Important decisions must be made quickly, but first it's essential to get centered. You need to gain a sense of control over your life. It helps to take a day off and find a restful place where you can be alone or with your partner. It's vitally important to allow yourself to relax because relaxation puts you in touch with your own inner strength and resources. This will help you to clear your thoughts and come to an appropriate decision.

The exercise on the following pages will help your conscious mind to unwind. By breathing deeply, you can calm your heart and your mind. Then you can begin to find peace, and this will help you to weather this storm.

You can read the following exercise into a tape recorder. The reading should be done in a slow, calm, rhythmic voice, emphasizing approximately every third syllable. (By using your voice in this way, you encourage the heart to take a steady, slow rhythm which quiets the mind and the body.) You may prefer to ask someone else to make the recording for you. The advantage of a recording is that you will be able to listen to it again and again, whenever you need to relax. Some people like to listen as they are falling asleep (it's very helpful if you have trouble sleeping) and then again as they are awakening. It's perfectly okay if you fall asleep while listening to the tape; it still works on your subconscious mind.

If you don't want to bother making your own tape, you may prefer to purchase one of the many relaxation tapes which are now available in many book and record stores. A good one is *Self Healing and Health Maintainance* by Dr. Lee Pulos.

Relaxation Exercise

Begin by turning off the lights. Take off your shoes and lie down on your back on a bed or comfortable mat. If you prefer, you can relax in an armchair. Cover yourself with a blanket, or if it's too warm, just keep one nearby, in case you want it later. Loosen any clothing which may constrict your breathing. Now close your eyes and relax. . . .

Inhale through your nose. As you draw the air into your body, feel it filling your lower abdomen, like a balloon. Hold your breath until it becomes a bit uncomfortable, and then exhale through your mouth, feeling the air gradually leaving your abdomen. I'm going to pause now for 3 minutes to allow you to take at least 10 of these nice deep breaths. Remember to inhale and bring the air all the way down to your lower abdomen. Feel it expanding like a balloon. Hold your breath until it becomes a bit uncomfortable, and then exhale through your mouth. (Pause for 3 minutes.)

Now, bring your attention to your feet. As you inhale through your nose, imagine your breath going all the way down to your feet. Then, as you exhale through your mouth, imagine that you are breathing away all the tension in your feet. (Pause 10 seconds.)

Repeat this same procedure with your calves (pause 10 seconds after naming each body part). . . . thighs. . . . genitals. . . . abdomen. . . . chest. . . . upper arms. . . . lower arms. . . . hands. . . . butt . . . . lower back. . . . small of your back. . . . area between your shoulder blades. . . . shoulders. . . . back of your neck. . . . scalp. . . . brain. . . . top of your head. . . . forehead. . . . eyebrows. . . . eyes. . . . nose. . . . cheeks. . . . lips. . . . jaw. . . . tongue. . . . throat.

Now I'm going to count slowly, from 7 to 1, and as I do, you'll feel yourself becoming more and more relaxed. Seven. . . . very deeply relaxed. . . . six. . . . very deeply relaxed. . . . five. . . . very deeply relaxed. . . . four. . . . very deeply relaxed. . . . three. . . . very deeply relaxed. . . . two. . . . very deeply relaxed. . . . one.

All right. Now imagine yourself outdoors in a very peaceful place (it may be imaginary or real). See yourself there. Feel the air. Is it warm or cool? Is there a wind? Are there odors? Listen to the sounds. (Pause

10 seconds.) Look all around you, observing the details of the place. Relax. I'll give you a minute to just enjoy being there. (Pause one minute.)

(If you're just doing the Relaxation Exercise, stop here and proceed to the last paragraph. If you want to do a visualization as described on page 45, please continue reading.)

Now you're going deeper and deeper, but you will not lose consciousness entirely; whenever you wish, you may choose to stop this process. But for as long as it feels deeply good and right, you will ask your conscious mind to step aside. Just relax. Ask your intuitive mind to take control. Trust your intuitive mind to take you lovingly where you need to go.

And now, I'm going to count again from 7 to 1, and as I do, you'll feel yourself becoming more and more relaxed. Number seven. . . . very deeply relaxed. . . . six. . . . very deeply relaxed. . . . five. . . . very deeply relaxed. . . . four. . . . very deeply relaxed. . . . three. . . . very deeply relaxed. . . . two. . . . very deeply relaxed. . . . one.

And now you are completely relaxed and peaceful. There is a white light encircling you and protecting you, so that only the good can enter. You are completely protected. Completely protected.

(Now you can go on to read one or more of the following visualizations. Or you may prefer to write your own. When you're finished, read the following.)

Now I am going to count from 1 to 7, and then you will find yourself returning to your waking consciousness. Your head will be clear and you'll feel more at peace with yourself, and better able to function and make decisions. You'll feel as if you were just awakened from a nice, refreshing nap. Number 1. . . . 2. . . . 3. . . . 4. . . . 5. . . . 6. . . . 7. Now you can stretch and yawn and open your eyes. You're wide awake Wide awake!

Use of Visualization

Too often we try to make decisions with only the conscious mind and we forget that we are complex creatures and that true satisfaction comes when we can listen to the needs of the heart and the spirit as well as the mind. So the best decisions and the deepest healings come from a blending and merging of all the levels of our total being. Visualization helps us to tap into these other levels.

Deep relaxation is the first step in the process of visualization, so you'll want to begin by using the Relaxation Exercise described on page 40, which will help your conscious mind to unwind. Some people think they cannot visualize, but anyone who has ever daydreamed or had a fantasy about something they wanted or feared has visualized. Just let your imagination go and follow its lead. It doesn't matter whether you see pictures or just idly imagine, sense, or hear things. Put your rational mind aside and allow your subconscious or intuitive thoughts to emerge.

Whenever you're given instructions in a visualization, just take the first image or thought that pops into your mind, whether or not it makes sense or seems important. Tell your conscious mind to step aside. Don't allow it to censor the material that the subconscious is giving to you. Try not to be preoccupied with whether or not your experience is real. It doesn't matter!

Begin by reading and then select the visualizations which best apply to your situation (see pages 44-47 and 93-97). These visualizations are given as models; don't hesitate to rewrite them. Put them into your own words and make them feel like your own. Then ask a good therapist or your partner or a close friend to read the Relaxation Exercise and your selected visualizations aloud as described on page 40.

If you use a tape recorder, be sure to pause at the designated times. If someone is reading it aloud, they should follow the same breathing and relaxing instructions and try to tune into their own inner guidance. Then you can describe what you are seeing aloud, and they can follow along and guide you, using their own judgment about what to say and how long to pause.

If you like, both you and your partner may lie side-by-side while the pages are being read.

Visualizations:

In Ten Years Time

This visualization is short and simple, but it has helped many women to decide whether to have an abortion or to keep their baby.

See yourself walking down a long corridor. You are walking forward in time, and at the end of this hallway, you will see yourself in ten years' time if you decide to keep this baby. (Pause 2 minutes.)

Now go back to the beginning. (Pause 10 seconds.) You will see another corridor. Go down this passageway, and at the end you'll see yourself in ten years if you do not have this baby. (Pause 2 minutes.)

Now return to the beginning, and you'll find a little room with a comfortable rocking chair. I'd like you to sit in this chair, and reflect on what you've seen. Just relax and rock yourself. (Pause 3 minutes.)

Visualization With Baby

The following visualization may be used when the woman and/or man would like to make contact with the entity which would be their baby. It can also be used after an abortion, if there is need to make peace with the entity.

And now, a special rose-colored light is surrounding the small being in your womb. (Pause.) There is a cord of light going from this being into the higher realms, where its soul consciousness resides. (Note: If this is being read after an abortion, substitute this sentence: I would like you to concentrate your attention on contacting the soul of the being that would have been your baby.)

You have the ability to speak to this being, and to give him or her permission to speak to you. Remember to breathe deeply and to relax your body. If tension gathers in some area, stop and breathe deeply into that part of your body. . . . relaxing. . . . allowing the tension to ease away.

Now call this being to you. If you have a name, use it. If not, just call "baby" or "being" or whatever you like. Call, and then wait in silence, breathing deeply, listening with your inner ear and feeling with your total being. Perhaps you will see or hear or sense a person speaking to you. It may be a child or an adult.

Feel the connection that exists between you. Now is the time to say or ask whatever you like. Then listen quietly, with an open heart and mind. Don't think about it; just pay attention to the first thing that comes into your mind. As if in a dream, you may hear or sense an answer from this being. (Pause 3 minutes.)

All right. When you feel ready, say goodbye. If you like, thank this entity for coming to you.

In times of need, many of us find ourselves wishing we could seek the counsel of an older, wiser person, who would offer some kindly advice, based on their long years of experience.

The subconscious mind is highly resourceful and if given a chance, will produce just such a person for you. Don't worry about whether your experience is 'real' or not. If the advice you receive feels good to you, then follow it. If not disregard it.

After many years of guiding people through this and similar visualizations, I am still amazed by the real wisdom which emerges when the Wise Woman speaks. I've only experienced one instance in which such a being offered advice which was less than helpful. So keep an open mind and give it a try.

See yourself on a path which winds up a mountain. As you follow this path, look around you. Observe what's growing there. (Pause.) Now I'll give you time to continue on uphill, and I want you to stop just before you reach the top. (Pause 1 minute.)

Now, as you come over the top, you'll see the place where the Wise Woman lives. The path will lead directly there. I'll give you time to observe the place carefully. (Pause 1 minute.) Move a little closer and look at the door. What is it made of? What color is it? What sort of handle does it have? Is there a lock on the door? I'll pause while you examine it. (Pause 1 minute.)

Now knock on the door or ring the bell, and wait for her to come. (Pause.) She's at the door now. Look into her eyes. Observe her face. Take your time. (Pause 30 seconds.) Do you trust her? If you do, then put out your hands to her. (Pause.) Now she's leading you inside. Take time to look around her house. (Pause 30 seconds.)

Now she's sitting down with you. She tells you that you may speak freely. Her smile is warm and welcoming. You know that you can say anything to her; she's sure to understand. You can ask her whatever you like. Take your time, and listen thoughtfully to whatever she says to you. I'll give you 3 minutes to do this. (Pause 3 minutes.)

When you feel ready to leave, thank her. See yourself leaving the house. Now you're on the path again. You're climbing down the mountain. Continue down until you come to where you started.

The Sacredness of Life

Most of us do not want to abuse the privilege of life. We want to regard all of life with love and respect. How then can we reconcile having an abortion with loving life?

The Native American medicine men and women regarded all life as sacred: the earth, the corn, the animals, the rocks. They regarded them as mother, father, brother, sister—as family.

Yet death was no stranger to these people. A hunter might call upon the spirit of the stag he hoped to kill. He might speak of the deep respect he felt for the stag. He might ask the stag to show himself, because the hunter's family was in need of food. And after the kill, he would speak to the stag and thank it for its meat, and urge its spirits to return to the same woods so that it would provide fine meat for his children and his children's children.

I have killed animals in this way, and I've felt at peace with myself when I've done so.

The other way of killing is to make yourself hard and cold and indifferent. When you do this, you cut yourself off from caring. If you are indifferent toward an animal, part of you becomes indifferent toward everything else, because you have to close down your heart in order to kill this way.

* * *

I believe there are spirits out there, looking for appropriate parents. When you get pregnant, this can be seen as a sign that a spirit has come knocking on your door.

I think the kindest thing you can do is to speak to that spirit. In your thoughts and meditations, examine and weigh your circumstances and explore if there is any way that you might be able to open that door, even though this visitor is unexpected.

Try to let that spirit speak to you—through your dreams and visualizations. Try to understand why it has chosen you and what its needs are.

Of course, not everyone can get such messages. But *many* of us do. The dreams, intuitions, and feelings of the heart come through—but we're taught to ignore them. I'd like to encourage you to listen to these messages. Open yourself to them.

Your needs are real too. Be in touch with them. Have faith that you too are a part of the sacredness of life. If you can truly open yourself to a dialogue with this spirit, I am convinced that you will find that it cares about you as much as you care about it. You will find that a meaningful dialogue can take place through which you will reach a decision that will feel right to *both* of you.

Even if you can't or don't care to do this sort of thing (it may sound like nonsense to you), if you want to have an abortion, you can simply acknowledge that there was a potential for life which has been cut off, and there is a sadness in this ("as when a blossom wilts with the first snow"). Then you will be participating in the sacredness of life.

* * *

I have been privileged to know some wise old Indian people. The midwives have medicines for abortions. The practice is ancient. I try to imagine what one of these women would say if she were to use the medicine for abortion.

She might speak to the spirit of the baby and say, "Greetings, little one. Little sister. Little brother. Great wise ancestor. You want to come to our home. Maybe you think we would make good parents for you. Well, the food is short now. The winter was too long and the summer too hot. We have too many mouths to feed. My husband works too hard already. We can't open our home to you now. Try again later, little one. Or find a better place. Go in peace now. Go in peace."

Abortion Politics

Is an Abortion a Murder?

Murder is defined as killing a human being unlawfully and with premeditated malice.

If you define murder as killing, then yes, abortion is murder. And picking a flower is murder. And picking a stem of broccoli is murder. And killing a chicken is murder.

Have you ever killed a cow? It is a terrible thing to kill a large animal. There are many people who have chosen to live as vegetarians rather than commit such murders. For some, it is a religious precept.

Yet vegetarians do not call meat-eaters murderers. They do not try to pass legislation against the eating of meat.

Presumably, when those who are opposed to abortion refer to an abortionist as a murderer, they are using the definition given above. Yet I have never met anyone who chose to have or perform an abortion as an act of malice.

When does a life become a human life? Is it when the spermatazoa enters the ovum? If so, then the IUD which seems to work by preventing the fertilized egg from implanting on the wall of the uterus is a form of murder. (And there are those who would legislate against IUD's for this reason.)

For 8 weeks after fertilization (or 10 weeks from the last menstrual period) the cells will multiply and the life will be called an embryo. This life-form cannot be distinguished from other developing vertebrates.

After the 10th week from the last menstrual period (6 weeks after the missed period and 2 weeks before the end of the first trimester), the embryo becomes a fetus and takes on distinctly human shape. For some people, there is a significant difference between aborting an embryo and aborting a fetus. Certainly the Pro Life literature is aimed at trying to make people feel guilty for "killing a baby," and to support this position they show pictures of the fetus in the 12th week and later. Yet these are the same people who oppose early pregnancy testing, menstrual extractions (very early abortions), and early vacuum abortions. In Canada, they have contributed to the fact that Canada has the second highest rate of second trimester abortions in civilized countries.

The Pope has ruled that all abortions are murder. I will not argue with the Pope. If Catholics wish to define abortion in this way, that is none of my affair. I do object when they try to impose their religious values on others. I object when they imply that women who choose abortions and those who assist with abortions are doing so with premeditated malice.

In North America we are mixed peoples of varying cultural, religious and moral backgrounds. Each of us struggles to define what is sacred to ourselves. Often it is difficult to accept our neighbor's point of view.

I have friends who decided that they would never choose an abortion. They could not bring themselves to do such a thing. They wish that others would feel the same way—but they do not call them murderers if they don't. We respect and love one another, though our choices have been different.

But I have other neighbors who believe that anyone who has an abortion is a murderer. They sincerely believe that in opposing abortion they are protecting the rights of the unborn. They see themselves as protecting the sacredness of human life.

I struggle to appreciate their point of view. I struggle to let them have their own opinions and to live their lives accordingly.

I've always been a fence-sitter because I am able to see both sides of every issue. This has often been an advantage, making me a good arbitrator. But I knew that some day I would be forced to take a stand. Writing this book has forced me to do that, and I am grateful for the opportunity. Already I feel strengthened by having made a clear decision.

I realize now that people who call themselves Pro Life have avoided saying that they are anti choice. There is an element of Orwellian doublespeak in this. By calling themselves Pro Life, they are implying that others are anti life. And they are avoiding the fact that thousands of healthy adult women have died as a result of illegal abortions and late abortions that were caused by women not having access to legal, safe, affordable, early abortions.

I believe that the philosophy of so-called Pro Life is a dangerous attitude which I must oppose. Throughout history innocent people have been oppressed by zealots, seeking legally to impose their moral values at the point of the sword. If they are allowed to do this, many of the other rights which women have struggled to achieve will also be in jeopardy.

Politics in the United States

Neither Church nor State prohibited abortion until 1803 when Britain passed an antiabortion law, with the U.S. soon following. In 1869, Pope Pius IV declared all abortions to be murder. It seemed to be part of a crusade against women's rights at a time when the women's suffrage movement was growing, and voluntary motherhood implied approval of sex for pleasure. At the same time, the male-dominated medical profession (which barred women from medical schools) was putting pressure on midwives to end their traditional practice of midwifery and abortion.

During the ensuing years, abortions were still performed, but illegally and often at great danger to the women receiving them. Abortionists were criminals. Abortions were available only to the rich who could afford to go to foreign countries to obtain safe abortions.

In the 1960's, the Women's Movement brought the abortion issue back into public awareness. In 1970, New York State passed a law allowing abortion on demand. In 1973, the U.S. Supreme Court interpreted the 14th Amendment's concept of personal liberty as being "broad enough to encompass a woman's decision whether or not to terminate her pregnancy." The Roe vs. Wade decision made it a private matter between a woman and her doctor. So a woman could choose to terminate her pregnancy through the end of her first trimester of pregnancy (the first 3 months, or up to 12 weeks after her last actual menstrual period.) Individual states could restrict second trimester abortions only when a woman's safety was jeopardized.

In July 1989, in the Webster vs. Reproductive Health Services Decision, the U.S. Supreme Court gave greater freedom to the states to restrict abortions. Roe vs. Wade was not overthrown, so the states were still required to allow a woman and her doctor to make the decision, but the details surrounding the abortion could vary from state to state. This would effect issues such as whether a teenage girl would require parental consent, whether a woman would have to have the consent of her spouse, and whether a waiting period should be required before a woman can obtain an abortion.

In October 1989, a California appeals court ruled that the state could not require a minor to get parental consent before terminating a pregnancy. Florida had a similar ruling. About two dozen states had questionable parental consent laws on their books. Some people claimed that the majority of pregnant teens did consult their families, but those who didn't often came from abusive homes and could be in danger if they told their parents. The California and Florida courts ruled that the Constitution protects a person's privacy and gives equal protection to minors. This ruling and others will be brought before the Supreme Court in the Spring of 1990.

In October 1989, for the first time in that decade, both houses of Congress changed their previous stance on abortion and approved bills which would finance Medicaid Assistance for poor women in the case of rape and incest and would expand funding for abortion services and international family planning programs. President Bush vetoed these bills.

1989 was an active year for abortion politics in the U.S. The Supreme Court had three Justices that were known to lean in the Pro-Choice direction and three that were known to lean in the so-called Pro-Life direction. One was undecided. The issue of abortion became very important for people. Many took public stands, including some Hollywood stars. Pro-choice politicians won three major races, campaigning on distinctly pro-choice themes. These were the governors of New Jersey and Virginia, and the Mayor of New York City.

On November 12th, more than one million people in 150 U.S. cities participated in 1000 pro-choice events as part of the National Mobilization for Women's Lives. In Washington, D.C. 300,000 people gathered for a pro-choice rally.

Pro-Choice leaders of Congress have introduced the Freedom of Choice Act of 1989. This bill would prohibit states from restricting women's rights to terminate a pregnancy prior to fetal viability or in cases where a woman's life or health are at stake.

Politics in Canada

Until recently, Section 251 of the Criminal Code of Canada required that abortions had to be performed only in approved hospitals (and, consequently, only under general anesthesia). Before obtaining an abortion, a woman had to run the gambit of a Therapeutic Hospital Board consisting of three physicians in addition to her own GP. These doctors had to determine whether having a baby would endanger her life and health. All this red tape led to unnecessary delays that resulted in Canada having the second highest rate of second trimester abortions in civilized countries.

Dr. Henry Morgenthaler became a renowned spokesman for early clinic abortions in Canada, and made his stance known in 1975 by openly defying the law. He did this by establishing an abortion clinic in Quebec. After numerous court cases, he was sent to jail for ten months. By the time he was released, a more liberal government was in power in Quebec (the Partie Quebecoise), and they opted to turn a blind eye to the federal government and Morgenthaler's clinic remained open.

For years Canadian women travelled to Quebec for abortions until 1983, when Dr. Morgenthaler opened another abortion clinic in Toronto, Ontario, and yet another in Winnipeg, Manitoba. Police raided these clinics and protesters harrassed, intimidated and verbally abused women who entered the clinics, but they remained open. Morgenthaler appealed to the Supreme Court of Canada.

For 19 months the Supreme Court deliberated until, on January 28, 1988, five out of seven justices declared that Section 251 of the Criminal Code violated a woman's right to life, liberty and security of person because it denied a woman's access to medical care and violated a woman's freedom of religion.

Morgenthaler was vindicated and all charges against him were dropped because 251 was declared unconstitutional since it denied a woman equal access to medical care according to where she lived, and because the Therapeutic Hospital Committee caused unnecessary delays that could endanger her health and welfare.

Meanwhile, a new abortion clinic was opened in Vancouver in November of 1988. Yet another clinic was opened in Halifax, but the government of Nova Scotia outlawed it. Not to be defeated, Morgenthaler has taken this case to the Supreme Court of Canada.

Abortion is no longer in the Canadian criminal code, though there are provisions against back-street abortions. However, a new bill, C-43, has passed through two readings in the House of Commons and is now in committee. It requires a third reading before it can pass. It states that doctors can perform abortions only if having the baby is a threat to the woman's health. It would criminalize abortion. Doctors could be indicted for performing abortions for "frivolous" reasons.

Most of this information comes from Norah Hutchinson, board member of CARAL, the Canadian Abortion Rights Action League.

Commentary

I worry that real women with real emotions and very difficult problems are being used as political pawns. I'd like to see more focus upon each actual human being (or potential human being) and less obsession with ideology. A woman seeking an abortion is often a person who is ambivalent. Excellent counseling should be provided *before* (and after) abortions. Many men will need this also. I think that this more than anything else would help to prevent many abortions which women later regret, and would certainly improve the quality of the lives of the people who have to make this painfully difficult choice.

I believe that this kind of counseling should be the major focus of any organization which sincerely wants to help a woman to make her own choice in this matter. Abortion clinics can be wonderfully supportive, but sometimes there is a built-in bias which assumes that abortion is the right choice. One of my clients had an abortion at a women's clinic and she was grateful for the support and friendly help she received. But later, she became severely depressed and found that she was unable to leave her house. She didn't realize that there was a connection with the abortion until we had been through several sessions when she suddenly said, "I'm punishing myself for killing my little boy. I wanted that child, but my boyfriend didn't, so I had the abortion. But I felt so terrible!" Tears welled up in her eyes. "No one ever asked me if I was sure I wanted an abortion."

I'd like to see more women's clinics and abortion clinics established, where unbiased, quality counseling was available. I'd like to see early pregnancy tests available to all women, and menstrual extractions legalized. (See pages 28 and 68.)

I suspect that many people believe that abortions should always be difficult to obtain and uncomfortable to endure, so that a woman will feel the weight of her decision, and will take it more seriously, and will feel guilty.

I've never known guilt to accomplish anything positive.

The
Abortion Procedure

Preparing for an Abortion

Before an abortion, be gentle with yourself. Admit that you're pregnant, and treat yourself with the care that a pregnant woman ought to have.

You and your partner (if you have one) may want to take the time to say goodbye to the spirit of the being inside your body. Ideally seek the aid of a counselor who works with visualizations. Some suggestions for visualizations are given on pages 44-47. These may be done alone or with assistance.

To make your body strong and your emotions stable, the following nutrients should be taken for several days before and after an abortion. Your partner (if involved) should also take vitamins B and C.

VITAMIN A — 25,000-50,000 I.U. per day, to aid in healing and to strengthen the adrenals to cope with stress.

VITAMIN B COMPLEX (or compound) — as described on page 31.

VITAMIN C WITH BIOFLAVANOIDS — 1000-5000 mg. per day, to prevent infection, repair blood vessels, and to alleviate stress. Bioflavanoids occur naturally in oranges, green peppers, rose hips, and many other foods which are high in vitamin C. They're important in the repair of blood vessels. You can purchase natural vitamin C with bioflavanoids.

VITAMIN E — 400-800 I.U. per day for tissue repair, and to alleviate stress by strengthening the pituitary and adrenal glands.

RESCUE REMEDY — as described on pages 32 and 112.

COMFREY, VALERIAN, YARROW AND PEPPERMINT TEA — This tea will help to build up your body's resources. Boil 3 cups of water. Add 1 Tbsp. comfrey leaves. Simmer 10 minutes. Remove from heat. Add 1 Tbsp. each of valerian root, yarrow flowers, and peppermint tea. Cover and steep for 20 minutes. Drink 1-3 cups per day. Use honey as desired. (Note: Comfrey builds the body's resistance by increasing the white blood cells. It contains allantoin which stimulates tissue formation and hastens wound healing. It also accelerates cell proliferation. Valerian relaxes the nerves and eases cramping. Yarrow cleanses the system and helps prevent infection. Peppermint settles the nerves and stomach, and is used for flavor. Some people get nauseous from valerian, so if this tea does not agree with you, leave out the valerian and substitute 1 Tbsp. of catnip or scullcap instead (these are also nervines). If valerian isn't used, then steep the tea for just 5 minutes. By the way, the drug valium is not related to valerian.

To Diminish Pain

The following are helpful for diminishing pain before, during, and after a medical abortion.

RESCUE REMEDY—as described on pages 32 and 112. Take 4 drops, under the tongue, every 10 minutes. Begin 20-30 minutes before the procedure, and continue 20-30 minutes after. It will help you to feel calm, centered, and less vulnerable.

CALCIUM—this works as an effective pain-killer. Take 800 mg. of calcium on the morning of the procedure. (Calcium with magnesium is fine, but not necessary.)

ARNICA — This is an effective homeopathic pain-reliever. It may be taken in pills of 6 x potency. These pills are available in some health food and herb stores, or they may be ordered from Standard Homeopathic, Box 61067, Los Angeles, California 90061.

ACUPUNCTURE ANESTHESIA—this is purely optional, but it can be used instead of other anesthesia during a suction abortion with flexible cannula. Even if a local anesthetic is used, the acupuncture will make it less painful. It also helps a woman to relax during a menstrual extraction. (These terms are explained on pages 70 and 71.)

The needles should be inserted at Spleen 6 and Conception Vessel 4, and then rotated fairly constantly during the procedure. (An acupuncturist will understand these instructions.)

What to Expect

Most abortions can be performed efficiently and with minimal emotional and physical trauma in a clinic setting. When you go for an initial exam and also on the day of the procedure, you will be asked to lie on an examining table with your hips at the end of the table and your feet up, resting in stirrups or your legs supported by knee pads.

The doctor or medical person will perform a bi-manual exam, inserting two fingers of one hand (covered with a surgical glove and lubricated with a lubricating jelly) into the vaginal canal, holding the cervix (the neck of the uterus, which extends down into the vagina) with his or her fingertips, and placing the other hand on top of the abdomen, to determine the size of the uterus.

Then the fingers will be removed and a speculum will be inserted. This is an instrument like a hinged double shoe-horn, which is used routinely during vaginal exams, to keep the vaginal canal open and allow a good view of the cervix (with the aid of a lamp). The speculum is usually cold (unless a thoughtful physician warms it in tepid water). It is lubricated with jelly and inserted. This usually does not hurt, particularly if the medical person is gentle and you can relax. It helps to breathe deeply and to concentrate on relaxing your mouth, jaw, chest, abdomen, and, of course, your vagina. If this is a pre-abortion exam, the speculum will soon be removed and the exam will be completed.

If you have come to have a laminaria inserted (see below), or if this is the day of the abortion, the cervix will then be grasped with a tenaculum (a long tweezer-like instrument that locks closed). This causes a slight pinch, but there are few nerve endings in the area, so the sensation is not remarkable. The tenaculum holds the cervix steady. Remember to breathe deeply, which brings more oxygen into your brain and body, which helps you to relax. It is tension which causes pain, so if you can concentrate on relaxing, and on breathing, then you are less likely to experience pain.

The necessity for anesthesia differs with each individual. Some women simply prefer to be knocked out altogether, and will opt for general anesthesia and a hospital procedure, even with an early abortion. But this does not actually eliminate the pain, since the cramping is there when you "wake up," and the trauma and risk are far greater (see below).

Most women prefer a clinic abortion, when available. The atmosphere is usually more relaxed, supportive and friendly. And relaxation is the key to pain prevention. If you are extremely nervous and anxious, then your cervix and vagina will probably be tight. The more you can relax through deep breathing and using the remedies on page 60, the less pain you're likely to feel.

A local anesthetic will usually be administered before an abortion (unless it is a menstrual extraction—see page 68). This is called a paracervical block and it involves injecting xylocaine or novacaine (similar to what a dentist uses) into the cervix at two points. This numbs the cervix and the uterus. The injection is relatively painless since the cervix is a muscle with few nerve endings. Local anesthesia will help numb the pain of having the cervix dilated. It's optional up to 10 weeks, and this will depend on your own needs (though some doctors will impose their needs on you). If you have a choice, some factors to consider are: Do you cramp with your menstrual period? Do you feel "uptight"? Do you know how to breathe as a method of pain control? Have you experienced natural childbirth? (You'll find that the same exercises which are used for childbirth are effective during an abortion.)

With early abortions (up to 8 weeks after the last menstrual period), very narrow tubes are inserted into the cervix and there is less need for dilation. After 8 weeks LMP, the tube which is needed is wider and it becomes necessary to dilate the cervix. The width of dilation will depend upon how far along the pregnancy is. Of course, the wider the dilation, the more the potential cramping.

One method of dilation is to insert a laminaria into the os (the mouth of the cervix). A laminaria is seaweed which is inserted dry and which then expands as it is exposed to body moisture, causing the cervix to expand. After the insertion you will be allowed to return home and then you'll come back in about 24 hours. You will probably experience some cramping pain as the laminaria expands. This can be eased by taking Tylenol (or some other brand of acetaminophen) or Tylenol with Codeine.

Another method of dilating the cervix is to use stainless steel instruments called dilators. These vary in size and are slighly curved on the ends. First the smallest one is inserted, which is about the diameter of a toothpick. Then progressively larger ones are inserted until the largest, which is about the width of a piece of chalk. This opens the cervix so that it is wide enough for the tip of the aspirator to enter the uterus.

Because the cervix is a muscle, and muscles cramp when they change size, a woman may experience what feels like very heavy menstrual cramping while the cervix is being dilated. Dilation usually takes less than two minutes. Breathing in short, quick pants can be helpful to alleviate this pain. It also helps to have a partner or friend to hold your hand.

The tip of the aspirator is then inserted through the open cervix into the uterus. The aspirator is a machine which consists of a vacuum-producing motor connected to two bottles to which is attached a hollow tube several feet long. At the end of the tube is a handle into which a variety of different-sized sterile hollow tips can fit. The size will depend upon the duration of the pregnancy.

The machine is turned on and the fetal material is removed by gently vacuuming the uterine walls. A curette (a rod-shaped instrument with a spoon-shaped end) may be used to gently scrape the uterine walls, to make sure all fetal material has been removed.

The aspiration generally takes 5 to 7 minutes and is a painless procedure. However, as the uterus is emptied, it begins to contract back to pre-pregnant size. Since it is a muscle, these contractions generally cause cramping. The cramping, often less severe than that felt during dilation, generally lasts 15-30 minutes after the procedure is completed. Recovery time with local anesthetic is usually about half an hour, after which most women may return home and resume normal activity (though I strongly recommend that you take at least a full day to assimilate this experience).

If an abortion is performed in a hospital, you will probably be given a general (or total) anesthetic. For most abortions, this is an unnecessary, expensive, and relatively dangerous complication. General anesthesia can worsen lung infections (including bronchitis and colds), it puts a strain on the kidneys (especially if the woman has a history of kidney disease or failure), it increases the chance of heart failure, and it requires the use of an anesthesiologist (which is costly). And the recovery time is longer.

When you wake up from general anesthesia, you may experience painful cramping as the uterus contracts to normal size. At this point, you may be offered "something for the pain," but drugs will just prolong the feeling of grogginess and lack of control. See page 60 for remedies for pain. The contractions only last 15-30 minutes. Again, Tylenol or Tylenol with Codeine can be used if needed. They are pain killers which have minimal side-effects.

For a description of abortions after 14 weeks, please see pages 73 and 74.

Medical Abortion Procedures

written with Dr. Jim Campbell*

In the past 20 years, several methods of performing abortion have been developed. Methods vary from one doctor to another, but the important thing is to find a doctor you can talk to, who will explain his or her methods to you (if you're interested). The method usually depends on how long the pregnancy has been allowed to develop. In general, the earlier the abortion, the safer and less painful it is. Also, earlier procedures tend to be less expensive. None of these methods should affect future fertility. Be sure to use birth control afterwards.

*NOTE: I worked with Dr. Campbell at the Country Doctor Community and Women's Clinic in Seattle, Washington. Over a period of three years he worked cooperatively with a group of midwives to develop an excellent home childbirth service. He was also in charge of the clinic's surgery services, which included abortions. I've asked him to describe these procedures, and I have made some additions.

Menstrual Extraction

This is the term used for very early abortion with the suction technique which removes the lining of the uterus (which normally detaches during the menstrual flow) and any pregnancy that might be there.

It was developed in the 1970s by self-help groups at the Feminist Women's Health Center in Los Angeles and elsewhere. It was a powerful example of women taking control of their own bodies. Women could be trained to do menstrual extractions without the aid of doctors. It is now illegal for anyone except a doctor to do this procedure.

A menstrual extraction is safe, simple, and relatively painless. But it must be done 5 to 6 weeks after the last menstrual period. This concurs with the date of the common pregnancy test (HCG), and therefore either an early blood test or early urine test must be taken.

This is the least traumatic form of abortion. It allows for the removal of the embryo while it is still truly in the embryonic stage, long before fetal development. Because it is not necessary to dilate the cervix, that painful procedure can be eliminated, and there is no need for local anesthesia (which is slightly painful), nor for general anesthesia (which is somewhat dangerous).

And since the uterus has barely had time to grow, there are no painful contractions when the uterus returns to normal size. Virtually the only pain is the pinching of the tenaculum, which makes it no more traumatic than the insertion of an IUD.

The exact procedure involves inserting a flexible plastic tube (a cannula) less than 1/4 inch (4mm) in diameter into the uterus. Suction is applied to the tube by attaching a regular syringe and drawing back the plunger. The tube is then moved back and forth while the suction gently removes the lining of the uterus.

Following this procedure, a woman can generally return home or to work after an hour or so of rest. She should watch for any undue bleeding, in excess of normal menstrual flow. She should also watch her temperature for any possible infection (which is rare). Temperature above 100 degrees is a danger sign.

There is a two to five percent chance that the pregnancy might continue. So this procedure requires that the woman return in two weeks for another pregnancy test, to be sure that the abortion was effective.

Suction Abortion with Flexible Cannula

From the time the urine pregnancy test becomes positive (about 6 weeks after the last menstrual period) until 8 weeks after the last menstrual period, it is possible to use suction through a flexible plastic tube (cannula) inserted through the cervix to perform the abortion. These tubes are small, the largest being about 1/3 inch (7mm) in diameter, and can be inserted into the uterus without the need for painful dilation of the cervix. The tube is then moved around in the uterus to remove all fetal material. This usually takes less than ten minutes. Blood loss from this operation is slight, generally less than one ounce. Pain produced is more than with a menstrual extraction, and it is customary to give the woman injections of local anesthetic such as novacaine or lidocaine around the cervix (paracervical block) to lessen the pain. Intravenous injection of Valium or a narcotic given just before the operation will also lessen pain and aid relaxation, but the grogginess produced by these injections lasts 4 hours or more, requiring the woman to have someone drive her home. Also she must rest for the remainder of the afternoon after the procedure. Complications from this operation are the same as for menstrual extraction, but they tend to occur more frequently.

Suction Abortion with Rigid Cannula

Suction Abortion with rigid cannula is used for pregnancies from 8 to 14 weeks past the last period. These cannulas are large—up to 1/2 inch (12mm) in diameter, and require that the cervix be dilated with special instruments. This stretching open of the cervix is very painful, and cannot be tolerated without good paracervical block or general anesthesia. The decision about whether to use a flexible or a rigid cannula will probably be made according to the size and shape of the uterus. During the later weeks, the uterus is larger, and there is more fetal material to be removed, so the rigid cannula is more likely to be used, and there is more danger of hemorrhage. Because of this, some practitioners give I.V. fluids during the operation to prevent shock. There is also the danger of tearing or puncturing the uterine wall. If the procedure is done gently, however, this should not happen. After the operation, the woman needs a full day to recover, especially if she had general anesthesia. Hospitalization is generally not necessary, though many doctors recommend it. Bleeding and fever need to be watched for at least a week afterward.

Dilation and Curettage (D&C)

D&C is similar to the suction procedure with the rigid cannula but the uterus is scraped out using curved metal scrapers called curettes. No suction is used. The cervix must be dilated beforehand (painful). Anesthesia complications, recovery time, and checking for postoperative complications are the same as for rigid cannula operations. D&C is generally used for pregnancies of 8 to 12 weeks duration from the last period. Many doctors will routinely curette out the uterus following a suction abortion, just to be sure they've removed all the material which could cause bleeding and infections later.

Dilation and Evacuation (D&E)

D&E is a relatively new method which can be performed from 14 to 24 weeks. It is used at the Oakland Feminist Women's Health Center in Oakland, California, but only for women who are up to 18 weeks past their last period. According to their literature, research has shown that having a D&E is safer than a saline or prostaglandin abortion (described below), and that having a D&E in a clinic is safer than in a hospital. In Oakland they require that women have an ultrasound to determine the age of the fetus, a complete physical exam. Then they insert the laminaria (see page 64) 12-24 hours before the procedure. Valium is given beforehand. An intravenous (I.V.) is inserted into the vein of the arm, as a preventative, in case of emergency. Then a cannula is used with suction. Then ovum forceps are used to remove the contents of the uterus and a curette is used to remove all tissue. The whole procedure takes about 15 minutes. In Oakland, a counselor stays with the woman throughout the procedure. Antibiotics are given to prevent infection, and pitocin is administered to contract the uterus back to normal size. Patients have less than a 1% complication rate.

Intrauterine Injection

After 12 weeks (3 months) past the missed period, the walls have become thinner, softer, and more spongy, making perforation and excessive bleeding more likely with the vacuum suction and D & C method. The fetus becomes too large to be safely removed by suction or curettage. At 16 weeks the uterus can be felt above the pubic bone (in the lowest part of the belly).

An injection is made with a long needle through the belly wall. The injection hurts little more than a routine "shot," so no anesthesia is needed. An abortion causing substance is injected into the amniotic sac which surrounds the fetus. Before 16 weeks LMP this sac is not large enough to be located accurately. Several hours after the injection, contractions will begin, causing the cervix to dilate and the fetus and placenta will be expelled. The contractions may be painful and some women require pain medication. When the fetus is passed, sometimes the placenta remains behind, which causes bleeding. To remove the placenta, the uterus may have to be curetted out (see D&C). Paracervical block or general anesthesia may be needed for this. After the uterus is completely empty, the woman is usually kept in the hospital for one day for observation (checking of bleeding and fever, etc.). After discharge she must observe herself for complications for at least one week.

The following substances may be injected:

SALINE—This is the older method, using a salt solution. Labor takes longer than with prostaglandin, and goes on longer before delivery. There is a danger that the salt will get into the bloodstream, which can cause a coagulation disorder which is very difficult to reverse and can lead to death. This method should not be used by women with liver or kidney problems, cardiac problems, or hypertension.

PROSTAGLANDIN—This is now the preferred method in most places. Prostaglandin is a hormone which appears naturally in a woman's body at the time of full term labor and delivery. It works more quickly and is not as dangerous as saline, but there are more side effects such as nausea, vomiting and diarrhea and a slightly higher rate of excessive bleeding and retained placenta. It causes quick, sharp contractions, which can tear the cervix unless precautions are taken. This method should not be used by women who have a history of convulsions, epilepsy, or asthma.

Other Methods & Techniques

Hysterotomy—This is the term for an incision into the uterus. It is like performing a mini-cesarean section, except in this case the fetus is to be aborted. This operation is usually reserved for pregnancies of 6 months duration when the fetus has been shown to be deformed through tests such as amniocentesis. General or spinal anesthesia is required.

Catheter—This is a flexible, hollow tube which is inserted into the uterus through the cervix, then left in place for several days. It irritates the uterus to cause expulsion of the fetus. It should no longer be used, as severe infection is common from this method and there are much safer methods available.

Follow-Up

Judging from the experiences of women I've observed, the hormones in your body will still be geared toward making a baby for as long as 30 days after the abortion. (This is true for natural miscarriages also.) So don't be surprised if you continue to feel weak, nervous, irritable, and vulnerable. You may find that your emotions are very close to the surface, and that the tears flow all too easily.

The following vitamins and herbs can help you to deal with the hormonal changes that your body will be going through.

VITAMIN B—Continue this vitamin until you feel stable.

COMFREY, VALERIAN, YARROW AND PEPPERMINT TEA—as described on page 60. Drink 1-2 cups on the day of the abortion. Then drink 1-3 cups per day until you feel normal. After the tension and cramping ease, you can omit the valerian, but continue the comfrey, yarrow, and peppermint for 1-2 weeks.

DONG QUAI (also spelled DOM KWAI or TANG KUEI, the botanical name is ANGELICA SINENSIS or ANGELICA POLYMORPHA)—this Chinese herb is considered the female equivalent of ginseng (a herb highly valued by the Chinese for its ability to strengthen male sex organs). Dong Quai is high in plant substances which resemble female hormones, and it's used to strengthen the female organs.

The dried root may be chewed, or taken in capsules as a powder, or the whole or granulated root may be prepared as a tea. You can nibble off a pea-sized piece of dried root once or twice a day, and allow it to dissolve slowly in your mouth. Or powder it and take it in a 00 capsule once or twice a day. Or make a tea using about 1 tsp. of dong quai root per cup of water and simmer at least 20 minutes, replacing the water as it evaporates. Drink 1-2 cups per day. Continue any of the above for about a month, then decrease gradually.

TO PREVENT INFECTION

For 2-4 weeks or until all bleeding has stopped:

Do not douche or use vaginal deodorants

Do not take tub baths

Do not use tampax

Do not have intercourse

Do not put anything into the vaginal area

Do not have an internal vaginal exam

After Anesthesia

If you have an abortion under general anesthesia, you may notice a feeling of disorientation which lasts beyond the time when the anesthesia should wear off. Mystics describe this effect as "puncturing the aura."

I've found that the best way to prevent or treat this condition is by lying under colored lights, as soon as possible after the operation. Colored lamps may be purchased at some health food stores. Many massage therapists give color treatments.

The best way to use colored light is to experiment with each color and see how it feels. Let intuition be your guide. Trust your own sense of how long to stay under each color. I think that you'll be suprised to find that the colors have a very strong effect, and that you will know exactly when you feel finished.

As a guideline, I would suggest the following regime, but please feel free to vary it according to your needs:

1) BLUE LIGHT should be used first, because it has a calming effect and it will soothe inflamed tissues. You can use it over your head for a few minutes and then over your uterus for 10-20 minutes.

2) INDIGO LIGHT is the color that appears in the rainbow between blue and violet; it's a bluish purple. In color healing, the seven colors of the rainbow correspond to the seven chakras or energy centers that are located along the spine. Indigo corresponds with the third eye, and is very effective in restoring the magnetic energy that surrounds the physical body (the aura). Use over the uterus for a few minutes, and then over the "third eye" for 10-20 minutes. Note: the most effective color treatments are done with German stained glass, but plastic gels are far cheaper and therefore more popular. If you do not have an indigo gel, a reasonable substitute is to use both the red and blue simultaneously.

3) GREEN LIGHT is the color of healing, and corresponds with the heart. Use this light wherever you feel tension and use it for as long as you like.

4) YELLOW LIGHT allows for deep relaxation and expansion,

such as you feel when you lie in the sun at the beach. Yellow corresponds with the solar plexus, below the breast bone and above the navel. Use it at the solar plexus or wherever else it feels good. You will probably feel energized by this color.

The sense of well-being, and the color that rises to the cheeks after this color treatment is remarkable. But even if you're feeling terrific, remember to rest and GIVE YOUR BODY AT LEAST A DAY TO RECUPERATE before resuming normal activities.

Note: For those who are skeptical about color treatments, it should be mentioned that a similar regime is used by Russian professional bicyclists, to help them recuperate quickly in between bike races.

Possible Complications

When technicians are well-trained and when women are encouraged to take an active part in their own care, complications are very rare. Complication rates increase when there are illegal abortions and abortions are done under conditions which are not sterile. Possible complications are:

1) HEAVY BLEEDING — may be caused by laceration (scratching) of the uterine wall or other complications. Heavy bleeding (more than twice your normal flow) often accompanied by heavy clotting might indicate that not all the fetal material was removed or that the uterus has not contracted down to normal size. It can occur during or after the procedure. However, some bleeding is normal for up to 3 weeks after an abortion, provided that it is not greatly in excess of a normal menstrual period.

Marion Toepke, Nurse midwife and Nurse-Practitioner, recommends massaging the uterus firmly while sitting on the toilet. This causes the uterus to expel pieces of retained material and it closes down the blood vessels. She and many other practitioners throughout North America have found the following remedies to be extremely effective. BE SURE TO GET PLENTY OF REST AND ELEVATE YOUR FEET. KEEP IN CLOSE CONTACT WITH YOUR DOCTOR, SINCE THIS CONDITION COULD LEAD TO A SERIOUS INFECTION OR EVEN DEATH.

The two main causes of heavy bleeding are:

A. *Pieces of Retained Material*

Occasionally, when an abortion is performed, a small piece of the placenta or other material may remain in the uterus, where it will cause irritation and possible infection. This can cause heavy bleeding, or bleeding which continues for more than seven days.

ANGELICA (root or seed)—This herb encourages the movement of pieces of retained material out of the uterus, perhaps by inducing contractions. (It's also used after births, when the placenta does not readily move out of the uterus.)

Angelica may be purchased as a dried root, or seeds, or powdered, or in tincture form. If you're using the root or seeds, boil 1½ cups of water and add 2 tsp. angelica and simmer 20 minutes in a covered pot. Or sprinkle 1 tsp. powdered angelica into the boiling water and simmer 5 minutes. Drink the full cup of tea. Or fill 4 gelatin capsules (00 size) with the powder, and swallow with warm water. If using a tincture, follow the instructions on the bottle. Whichever form of angelica you use, repeat the dosage 2 or 3 times per day, until the discharge stops.

B. *Uterine Hemorrhage*

If a blood vessel has been ruptured, there will be an extreme loss of blood. Other symptoms might be restlessness, cold and clammy skin, thirst, increased and thready pulse, rapid and shallow breathing and a drop in blood pressure, leading to visual disturbances, ringing in the ears or extreme weakness.

If you're hemorrhaging, you could go into shock and YOU SHOULD NOT BE ALONE. Take plenty of fluids and elevate your legs so that your feet are higher than your head. This helps get more blood and oxygen to your brain, which will help to prevent shock. CALL YOUR DOCTOR IMMEDIATELY, because hemorrhaging is extremely serious and could be fatal. But if one of the following remedies can be taken immediately, it will probably stop the hemorrhaging within 5-10 minutes.

SHEPHERD'S PURSE TEA—Cover 1 tsp. shepherd's purse herb with 1 cup boiling water and steep 5 minutes. One cup is usually enough, but use up to 4 cups in one day. The bleeding should normalize within the day.

CAYENNE—Take two 00 capsules of cayenne powder (available in grocery and herb stores) every half hour for up to 3 hours. 00 caps are empty gelatin caps, 00 size holds ¼ tsp.

2) INFECTION—may result from unsterile instruments, from lowered resistance, from douching or using a tampax or having intercourse before the uterus is fully healed. A temperature of over 100.5°, heavy cramping, nausea or vomiting are all danger signs that can warn of infection. This may occur in one out of every 1000 abortions.

3) PERFORATION — Perforations of the uterine wall are generally slight and will often heal by themselves. But a large perforation can damage the uterus and sometimes other internal organs and can lead to infection, hemorrhage or other complications. This may occur in about 2.3 of every 1000 abortions.

4) INCOMPLETE ABORTION—If any fetal material is not removed, this may necessitate a D&C (see page 72) to complete the abortion. Warning symptoms are a foul smelling vaginal discharge, cramping, nausea, vomiting, prolonged heavy bleeding, and infection. This may occur in about 1 out of every 1000 aspiration abortions.

After An Abortion

Stages of Grieving

Any death or loss tends to move through five distinct stages of grieving. In some cases, the woman may be so clear about what she wants that she can move through an abortion with a minimal sense of loss. Not everyone goes through all these stages, and it doesn't always happen in the same order, but it helps to have some idea of what to expect.

The loss associated with abortion is unusual because it has two distinct phases. The first phase comes after getting a positive pregnancy test. At that moment, most women feel a loss of control over the circumstances of their lives. There may be a serious identity crisis. If you choose to become a mother, you may be in danger of losing your career or your freedom or some concept of who you are. If you choose an abortion, you may feel a loss of your image of yourself as a loving and nurturing person.

And then if you do have an abortion, there is the loss of the potential baby. The loss of power over your body. The loss at having something taken from your body. And often there is a change in a couple's relationship that is a loss.

So for most women, there is much to grieve over. And yet, in some cases, this does not happen. Particularly if the woman (and her partner, if she has one) feels very clear about the unsuitability of becoming a mother at this time, and if she does not carry a heavy burden of guilt about her decision.

Abortion is a unique experience for each woman (or couple), and if it happens more than once it is likely to feel entirely different each time, because of the circumstances of that pregnancy, the circumstances of the relationship, and the circumstances of a woman's life at the time that she became pregnant.

So there is no way that anyone can predict how it will feel to you. But I would like to urge you to experience your feelings—whatever they are, no matter how intense or mild they may be. And please, try to find someone to talk to, someone you can share your feelings with because the feelings that are expressed will be released and will change and will eventually lead to acceptance. But the feelings that are blocked will stagnate and fester and, while you may look good on the outside, you will be a walking time bomb on the inside. And this will lead to irritability with the people you love, and all kinds of stress and tension and possible disease.

The Stages of Grieving are:

1) DENIAL — Our first reaction to loss is to protect ourselves from the shock. In the beginning, when your period doesn't come on time, its hard to believe that you may be pregnant. Particularly if you've never been pregnant before, it seems unthinkable that your body would suddenly start to function in such an unpredictable way. Even after a positive pregnancy test, many women do not think seriously about an abortion because they simply cannot believe that they are really pregnant. This is one of the causes of late abortions. And finally, even after the abortion, many women will return to work the same or the next day and try to pretend that nothing happened. *Please take time to assimilate this experience.*

2) ANGER—Sometime before or after the abortion, you'll probably feel a surge of anger. It may be directed irrationally toward some lady in the supermarket, or it may be a terrible resentment toward the father of the baby, or even toward your doctor. If you realize that anger is a part of the grieving process, it may help you to accept that emotion. Try to find a safe and effective way of letting off steam. This is *not* a good time to try to communicate! *After* you've released the anger (through running, swimming, chopping wood, or beating on a mattress), then I believe you'll find it much easier to communicate, and you'll probably feel a great weight lifting from your shoulders. (Please see page 89 on Releasing Emotions.)

3) BARGAINING—If this stage occurs before the abortion, you may find yourself pledging to work in an orphanage to make up for what you're doing.

If it's after an abortion, you may become very ill, or deprive yourself of something you really want, as a way of trying to even things out.

It's good to recognize this as a stage in your grieving process because you may find yourself making promises that you will later regret. Usually, bargaining is just a way of putting off the inevitable next stage. . . .

4) DEPRESSION—This is when you just let loose and cry your heart out. Even if you never wanted a child, there's still something very sad about having an abortion. For most women, this *is* a death. It *is* a loss. It *is* a sadness. At first they may deny this, but sooner or later it's likely to catch up with them.

I see many women who took their abortions lightly, but even 30 or 40 years later, they find themselves thinking, "How would my life be if I had that baby now?" Even then, it's not too late for them to express their grief, to cry for the daughter or the son they never had.

But too often the tears that aren't shed today are tucked away in some part of the body, only to emerge years later as pelvic inflammatory disease (P.I.D.) or a breast tumor, or uterine cancer. (Please see pages 87 and 88.)

And there are other sources of sadness. The violation to your body, changes in the relationship.

Most of us try so hard to look as if nothing is happening, that we fool ourselves. But the sooner you can allow yourself to feel the sorrow, the sooner you're likely to let go of the grief.

5) ACCEPTANCE—When you've allowed yourself to feel all your emotions, it will be much easier to relax and accept what has happened and move on with your life. It may take you five minutes to move from denial to acceptance. Or it may take years. Some people never accept the losses they experience.

Guilt and Grief

I'd estimate that one out of ten people who come to see me—for a wide range of emotional and physical problems—can trace the origin of their problems back to an abortion, or to giving up a child for adoption (or having been given up as a child).

This does not mean that all abortions and adoptions will lead to serious problems. Nor does it mean that these problems are insurmountable. But I have found that the people who make the best adjustments are usually the ones who are able to give full expression to their emotions as early as possible.

Many diseases are caused when we experience a death or loss and we don't know how to release the wellspring of emotions associated with that loss.

In their extensive work with cancer patients, Carl and Stephanie Simonton found that most cancer patients had experienced a series of stresses six to eighteen months prior to the onset of cancer, and had responded with a deep sense of hopelessness, of "giving up."

The stress which is caused by a serious loss will elicit a specific chemical reaction in the body. The pituitary gland (in the brain) will secrete a hormone which will trigger the adrenal cortex, which will in turn secrete another hormone that will mobilize the body for fight or flight.

When we hold back our emotions and keep everything too well under control, this often results in chronic stress, which produces hormonal imbalance. When this occurs, it can lead to high blood pressure, kidney damage, arteriosclerosis, and suppression of the immune system, which can result in chronic illness and even cancer.

So it's not necessarily the event, but rather the inability to grieve over the loss, which often causes emotional and physical problems in later life. For example, a woman who was diagnosed as having uterine cancer used visualization to discover the origins of her illness. In a light trance, she re-lived a pregnancy she had when she was 35. She wanted to keep the baby, but her boyfriend threatened to leave, and her mother told her she was crazy to have a child at her age, so she succumbed to the abortion. But her womb still longed for the child she never had. Yet outwardly, she just became depressed and the relationship deteriorated. When she was able to express her anger toward her mother and her boyfriend, this helped her to reactivate her self-defence system, and she was eventually able to cure the cancer through this and other natural healing methods.

Releasing Emotions

There may be people you need to talk to, and you may feel afraid to do that. You may need to face your mother's disapproval. Or you may be furious with your boyfriend or husband. You may need to tell someone off and shout and scream and cry.

Now I'm not suggesting that you go out and confront someone, because you can hurt people whom you may care about, and get badly wounded yourself. But if you keep your feelings bottled up inside, you may find you're suffering from a sore throat or headache or a variety of aches and pains. If you let these emotions build up without expressing them, you're going to be a nervous wreck or a time bomb, or else you might just go numb. Or maybe you'll lose interest in sex.

I know several women who, after one or more abortions, found that they no longer desired to have intercourse. Their fear of becoming pregnant again made it difficult to relax during intercourse. Some developed a mysterious vaginal itch or irritation or pain which disturbed them only during intercourse. Some harbored deep resentments toward the men who made them pregnant. For some, it just didn't seem fair that *their* bodies should be violated by an abortion. Some felt betrayed by their bodies. Some felt angry at the doctors who performed the abortions.

There is an alternative to carrying around all that emotional poison. You can find a way to express your anger—a way which involves your body. Anger stimulates hormones which elicit a "fight or flight" response from us, and when we "act civilized" instead of fighting or running, we suffer from a hormonal imbalance which leads to illness. So when we involve our bodies in expressing our anger, we relive the event vividly and thereby release that toxin from our bodies.

If you can find a safe way of releasing your emotions (especially your anger) you may feel exhausted for a few hours or even a day or so, but then you'll find your energy and your positive feelings toward life coming back with a new surge. Negative feelings seem to float to the top like oil on water, and until they're released, they suppress the positive feelings that lie just below the surface.

So, how do you release your feelings? Ideally, find a good therapist who does emotional release work. But if this isn't available to you. . . . Many people like to go for a drive alone and roll up their windows and scream their heads off. But please, drive carefully! Find a place where you can easily pull off to the side, because tears often follow rage, and it's hard to drive when the tears are welling up in your eyes.

I know one women who goes swimming and screams underwater. Many people are learning to use a tennis racket or their fists or an 18-inch length of heavy-duty industrial rubber hose to beat on a mattress. Others are using punching bags or running or playing racquet ball or chopping wood. Just concentrate on the object of your anger and find a way to release that anger and frustration *without hurting anybody*. Because once you've released all that tension I think you'll find you can communicate a lot easier with the person you need to talk to, because your message won't be so loaded. In any case, I think you'll find *yourself* a whole lot easier to live with.

A Funeral

Your egg and his sperm came together, and a small thing began to take on a life of its own. Life is miraculous. In time, a live baby could have formed.

What you have now is not a baby. Why make a fuss?

When a medical abortion is performed at an early stage, what is removed looks like clots. If requested, most doctors will give this to you. Though it doesn't look like much, for some people, disposing of these remains in a thoughtful way helps to affirm the sanctity of all of life, and seems far preferable to throwing it in the garbage (which is what hospitals and clinics generally do).

With a later abortion, there is truly a fetus, or even a baby, or— what is still harder—parts of a fetus or a baby, It is common practice for clinics and hospitals to spare the mother the pain of having to deal with this. To dispose of it as rapidly as possible. To remove any sign of what has been done.

I believe this may be a mistake. But it's a very personal choice. You may not want to look at what has been removed. (It may be good to ask someone who has seen it what to expect.) Particularly if it is a late abortion, it may be best to bring a suitable container, and then dispose of the container in an appropriate way without actually looking at the contents.

If you want to keep the remains after an abortion, you may find that medical workers are insensitive about this. In some places, the fetus is routinely placed in formaldehyde and sent up for a biopsy. What possible justification there is for this, I cannot comprehend. But if enough people protest these procedures then eventually the rules will change. We still live in a death denying society, but consciousness is changing rapidly.

So, if it feels right to you, and if the circumstances permit, then find a way of keeping the embryo or fetus, in order to have a ceremony with it. I've found that having the actual body, or even a fragment of that body, makes the mourning more intense and more real and serves as a catalyst in enabling you to cry out all your tears and be able to get on with the stuff of life.

But if you don't have the embryo or fetus, try to create something which symbolizes the baby that you might have had. One woman made a little baby out of clay. Another made a small flowered pillow. Yet another couple used an egg to symbolize the child: they held the egg, slept with it, and sent it the vibrations of love which they would have wanted to give their baby.

Whatever symbolizes the baby for you, keep it with you for an hour or a day and cuddle it, hold it in your arms, sing to it, tell it all the things you would have wanted to have said to that baby.

And then, when you feel truly ready, say goodbye to it. And perform a burial, or some other ritual that feels complete to you.

It brings up a lot of sadness to acknowledge this death through such a ritual, but that sadness is a part of life, and if we pretend not to feel it, something may begin to die inside. By allowing the tears to flow, we participate in life, we affirm our inner being, and we can genuinely say goodbye and begin to move toward accepting and resolving the loss which has occurred.

Further Visualizations

On the following pages you will find visualizations which will help you to come to terms with the abortion.

When someone dies, their loved ones often hold onto them, unable to let go, unable to accept the death. Psychics often report that this is draining to the spirit of the one who has died. It happens often when the person who is still alive carries a burden of guilt toward the one who has died, and somehow feels responsible for the death. Frequently such people will have very convincing dreams or visions in which the person who has died appears to them in a flood of beautiful white light and tells them that they are at peace and not to worry about them.

Since women who have had abortions (and sometimes men) often carry a burden of guilt, their energy will sometimes pull on the spirit of the "baby." These women experience nightmares and nervous tension or headaches or fatigue. Of course, their burden of guilt is only detrimental to the spirit of the "baby," and so anything which can help these women to release their guilt will, in turn, release the spirit.

For example, one woman went to Japan after an abortion and she was approached by a Buddhist priest who said, "You have had a difficult experience. Perhaps the death of a baby?" When she acknowledged that she had had an abortion, the priest said, "You must let go of this baby. You are hanging onto it and preventing it from moving away from you."

Releasing the Spirit

See this entity as a child. Your child. You are walking along a path, and the child wraps its little hand around your finger. There is a sweet rapport between you.

As you walk, there are scenes on either side of the path, depicting events that might have occurred in your life with this child. Observe these events for as long as you care to. Allow your feelings to surface. (Pause for two minutes. If you are with the person who is doing the visualization, ask to her to describe what she is seeing. Ask occasional questions to draw her out. After she describes one scene, encourage her to continue on the path and to describe any other scenes she may see. Probably these scenes will invoke mixed responses; joy and tears. Allow the tears to flow. They are cleansing. Continue doing this until you feel that she is finished.)

Now you are approaching the end of this path. You know that your small companion must go on without you now. You have packed a little suitcase for your child. You set it on the ground and open it up and inside are three special, magical gifts. As you give each gift to your child, watch the expression on his or her face. There is something that symbolizes your love (pause for 15 seconds); there is something for protection (pause for 15 seconds); and there is a gift to give strength for the long journey (pause for 15 seconds).

Then your child offers a gift to you (pause for 15 seconds).

I want you to know that if you choose to, you will be rejoined with this child when you die.

Now you can say whatever is in your heart, whatever you long to say to this child. (Pause for 1 minute. If you are with the person, let her speak out loud.) Then give the child time to speak to you, or to radiate its essence to you. (Pause 1 minute.)

Now it is time to say goodbye. (Pause 1 minute.) Open your arms and let go of this precious being. Bless it, and send it on its way. Feel the love radiating between you. See this spirit moving toward the white light.

Let go. Let go.

The Uterus as a temple

Many women who have abortions describe feeling betrayed by their bodies, distrustful of their sexuality, alienated from their female organs. The following visualization is a powerful tool for regaining the full potency of your uterus, your femininity, and your body.

You're coming into the temple. Look around you. It's a sacred place. (Pause.) But something disturbing has happened.

You are the High Priestess here, and you have the power to purify this place and to heal the wounded. This temple lies at the womb center of your spiritual, physical, and emotional total being, and it is sacred and beautiful.

Now you're bringing lots of beautiful, colorful flowers, with all their exuberant female genitalia intact. (Pause 15 seconds.) You're bringing lots of colored candles, and lighting them in your temple. (Pause 15 seconds.) And now you're bringing a gift, something which will restore the energy in your temple. (Pause 1 minute.)

Fill your temple with the color violet, and feel your connection with the Divine Cosmic Source. (Pause 10 seconds.) Fill your temple with the color blue, and feel your connection with Spirit. (Pause 10 seconds.) Fill your temple with green, and feel the healing energies filling this sacred place. (Pause 10 seconds.) Fill your temple with pink, and feel the love flowing through your temple, restoring it to perfect glowing health. (Pause 10 seconds.) Fill it with yellow, and feel the power in your womb. (Pause 10 seconds.) Fill it with orange, and feel the goodness of your sexuality. (Pause 10 seconds.) Fill it with red, and feel your connection with the Earth Mother. (Pause 10 seconds.)

Let this temple be full of sparkling rainbow lights. You are whole. Your womb is full of beauty. Use it wisely and carefully. Honor it, and keep it sacred.

Healing the Relationship

After an abortion, a couple may feel traumatized (see page 21). Here is a way to help restore your spirit. This visualization may be done with only one person, but it's best when both are present. Then you can lie on your backs alongside each other. If you like, you can hold hands.

Picture the womb of this woman as a temple. (Pause 30 seconds.) Something hurtful has happened here. Come into the temple and make a peace offering; bring something to restore the beauty of this place. (Pause 1 minute. If desired, the couple can each describe aloud how the temple looks, and what sort of peace offering they brought.)

If you wish to have another baby in the future, perhaps you'd like to bring in a special cradle, as a promise for the future.

Now see yourselves standing in the temple together, facing one another. Take your partner's hands and look into each other's eyes. Feel the trust and love flowing between you. (Pause 15 seconds.) Now feel the spirit of the baby and hold it in the aura which flows between you and your partner. Let it feel embraced and loved by both of you. Always remember that the love between you has created a new spirit, and nothing can take that away. You may choose, in the future, to bring it into flesh again, or you may not. The choice is up to you. This spirit is still with you, and can return later if you ask. But even if you choose not to have a child, you can still affirm your connection with this spirit, which is part of the creative power of your relationship. Now feel that spirit between you. Feel yourselves merging with it. Feel it as an extension of both of you. Feel how you are both united in this spirit. (Pause 2 minutes.)

And now, a wise being is approaching. This figure carries an urn of pure white light. The urn is being held over all of you and the white light is streaming over you. Feel the cleansing power of this pure white light, carrying away your guilt, your sorrow, your anger, your resentment, your pain. (Pause 1 minute.)

Now this wise being holds out its hands toward you and you can feel pink light coming from its heart and radiating directly into your hearts, healing the pain, making you whole again, whole within yourselves, and whole within the relationship. (Pause 1 minute.)

And now, the spirit of your baby is leaving with this wise being. Trust that it will be well cared for. Say goodbye for now. (Pause 1 minute.)

Let yourselves feel the beauty and sanctity of the womb in which you stand. (Pause 1 minute.) Then see yourselves leaving this temple, hand-in-hand, feeling renewed and full of light.

How
Some People Cope

Stories of Coping

While I was working on this book, I received a phone call from my friend, Cathrin Leslie, a midwife, in Vancouver. She described a wonderful delivery she had just done for a woman who gave up her child for adoption.

The adoptive parents were at the baby's birth. Cathrin was in the process of writing this story for her own book, and she generously allowed me to include it in this book.

In addition, there are stories that I wanted to tell about how women and couples have coped with being unexpectedly pregnant.

Pretty Big Favor
by Cathrin Prince Leslie

Ann was the loving single mother of a robust four-year-old boy. She had her third abortion at the request of her boyfriend in the false hope of rectifying their relationship. After the abortion, Ann said, "I felt that I had thrown away something precious."

Three months later Ann found herself pregnant again. She and her son moved away from their small home town, and she began to investigate adoption. She was certain that she did not want to parent this child. She inquired about the government agency and talked to lawyers about private adoption. She was given profiles of "approved" parents who were waiting for a baby. But anonymity was the rule.

When she was 6½ months pregnant, Ann came to me, seeking midwifery care. During prenatal visits we explored the various options available. Ann stayed firm in her decision to give the baby up for adoption. Her ambition was to find parents for this baby who were interested in being at the birth.

Ann had given birth at home and had also watched her nephew being born at home. Both these experiences convinced her that the energy of birth was "heart-opening," and would give both the parents and this baby the best start possible. It was important to Ann that this baby's first hours and days were not spent in a nursery without parents and loving skin-to-skin contact.

Finally an opportunity came. We heard about a couple who wanted children and wanted to be at the birth. We arranged to meet with Bonnie and James. James had a twinkle in his eye that signed him as a good dad. Bonnie's sincerity shone through her excitement about the all-but-lost prospect of mothering a newborn. Her tubes were blocked with scar tissue from problems which she thought had developed from the use of a Dalkon Shield IUD. She had no hope of ever conceiving.

Then a great process of discovery began. They examined needs, desires, fears, backgrounds and compatibilities. Everything from breastfeeding to education was discussed. Tears and laughter flowed. Plans were changed and remade. It wasn't easy, but it was happening and it was exciting.

The option of changing her mind was often discussed and always left open, but Ann was steadfast. She talked about feeling love for the baby and yet not feeling a maternal bond. "It was as though there was a nurturing love coming to this baby from somewhere else." Meanwhile Bonnie and James and even their friends were literally having dreams and visions of holding and loving this baby.

Bonnie pumped her breasts every four hours for over a month before the birth, in preparation for breastfeeding. This caused her breasts to develop signs of pregnancy and the initial secretions of milk. James was continually supportive. Preparations for a home birth were made. Once everything felt right, they began the legal procedures.

All three "parents" were in agreement that Ann would have ongoing contact with the child.

Ann's due date drew closer and passed, but not for long. Labor began at night and as dawn arrived, Ann's contractions were strong and rhythmic. Bonnie and James arrived to give support, massaging and holding Ann, so that all three were working toward the birth of this baby. Everyone was tremendously vulnerable. Ann felt that Bonnie's presence encouraged her labor. It wasn't long before the baby was crowning.

Both Bonnie and James were able to touch baby Lena as she was born, and Bonnie helped to pass her into Ann's arms. Ann said, "She was so beautiful, but I knew that she wasn't really mine. It felt so good to hold her and make that loving connection with her, especially knowing that I could do this and not feel guilt in handing her over to those beautiful people who are her parents."

After several minutes, Ann passed Lena to her new mother who, exploding in ecstasy, welcomed her to her bosom, to her joy, to her tears, and to her love. Ann looked on. "It made me feel so fulfilled; that I had given them this gift of life."

When the time was right, Bonnie and James went home with their baby only half a day old.

The next day we formed a milk bank through which lactating

women, including Ann, supplied baby Lena with breast milk for her first month. (After that, she drank supplementary goat's milk.) Lena was fed at Bonnie's breast and received the milk through a tiny tube. (This apparatus is called an axicare kit and is available from La Leche League.) Bonnie began taking a 3-week course of metochlorpramide, a drug which encourages the production of prolaction, to increase her milk supply. It worked.

As this story is going to press, baby Lena is nine weeks old and Bonnie is successfully breastfeeding her. Bonnie and James are as enchanted with her as ever. She seems to be a well-adjusted baby. Ann has visited Lena several times and she has no regrets about her decision.

When I told my six-year-old daughter about what had happened, she was quiet for a while and then responded, "That's a pretty big favor for Ann to do for Bonnie, isn't it Mom?"

(Commentary from Joy: While it is unconventional to allow the birth mother to have an ongoing relationship with her baby, these three parents have broken with convention and intend to allow Ann to maintain that contact with Lena. Admittedly, it is a potentially volatile situation, but so is custody arrangement. It used to be considered better for one parent to have custody and for the other parent to virtually disappear. Now joint custody is becoming popular, and when the parents can get along well enough to maintain it, the children benefit from having the love and presence of both parents, even though it is sometimes disruptive. I believe that baby Lena will stand an excellent chance of not feeling abandoned by Ann as she grows older. She may even feel doubly blessed.)

* * *

Lydia

Lydia didn't say much during the class, but her appearance was striking—particularly the red and white Hawaiian dress. I stood by the door, saying goodbye to the students as they left, and I saw her lingering nearby, grasping her little handbag like a frightened child. Then she left. Perhaps she wanted to ask something, but didn't have the courage.

Two weeks later she called; she wanted to see me right away. I made the time for her. She arrived and sat at the edge of the couch, almost trembling. "I'm pregnant," she announced, "and I don't know what to do. I'm a single parent and my little boy is six years old. I have a boyfriend, but it's not a strong relationship. He doesn't like abortions, and neither do I. But I don't want to raise another child alone. I'm 28, and I want a career for myself."

As so often happens, she said, "I was just about to get my tubes tied when I got pregnant."

I suggested that she might want to try to contact the spirit of the entity inside her. She agreed. So I asked her to stretch out on the couch so that I could induce deep relaxation. Before she closed her eyes, she told me, "I've had this image of going to a lake and playing with two little girls. I don't know where it comes from, but I feel a lot of love for those little girls. I don't know if they represent my sisters, whom I'm very close with, or my own daughters, or myself as a child. But there are two of them and I see myself as an adult."

I responded that perhaps an understanding of this image would come when we did some visualizations.

As she became deeply relaxed, I asked her to allow her spirit to float up toward the heavens, and then to call for the spirit of the entity inside her. Instead, she reported that she was going through a tunnel, and I recognized this symbology as the beginning of a past-life experience.

"I see two attractive, happy young women," she said. "They're pushing two beautiful little girls in carriages. They're laughing and having a good time."

Then she was silent for a while, and a troubled look crossed her face. "I don't understand. I just get a horrible image of a muddy boot crushing a little doll." Then she started to cry. I suggested that she remove her emotions from the scene and just watch from a distance, as if from a cloud. She attempted to do this, but her whole body was wracked with sobs.

Little by little she uttered disconnected phrases that suggested that one of the women was brutally raped "and the child died—in the storm."

"After that," she continued, "the woman was grey. She had been pink, but now she was grey. She wore a big hat on her head, with a scarf under the hat, and she never smiled and she never cried."

"Lydia," I said, gently, "I want you to let your spirit rise again, and let it become one with your higher consciousness, where all things are known. Let me know when you feel that connection."

After a minute, she said, "All right."

"Ask your higher consciousness, 'What was the lesson to be learned in that lifetime?'

She responded immediately. "Not to close off. Even when you're hurt, don't close off. The woman became grey. She had been pink, but she became grey, and she died inside,"

"And was that woman you?" I asked.

"I think so."

"All right," I continued, "now I want you to feel your spirit coming down to your present body. And I want you to see yourself walking down a long corridor. You are walking forward in time, and at the end of this hallway, you will see yourself in ten years' time if you decide to keep this baby. Now describe what you see."

"There is lots of pink light. I have a good relationship with my daughter, and it feels fulfilling. My son isn't there — perhaps he's off to school. But that feels all right."

"And what about your work?" I ask.

"Oh, that's the same. You know how it is; just as you achieve one goal, you've already set a new one for yourself."

"All right," I respond, "now I'd like you to go back to the beginning of that corridor, and you'll see another corridor, and I'd like you to go down that hallway, and at the end you'll see yourself in ten years if you give up this baby."

"It's grey," she responded. "There are lots of books, and reading glasses. But it all feels kind of empty. That's strange; it's like the difference between the grey and pink, with that other woman."

When Lydia returned to her waking consciousness, I hugged her, and she clung to me for a long long time.

Kathi and Paul

I first met Kathi at one of my two-day workshops for women on abortion. She's a tall, slender redhead. She was furious because the doctor who performed her abortion had been negligent and left behind some of the fetal material, so she had to return for a D&C. That meant having to undergo two abortion procedures within a month.

Since the abortion, Kathi felt cut off from her female organs. She felt betrayed by them. She resented having gotten pregnant when she had no intention of doing so. She resented having to go through a painful and degrading operation. She was furious at Paul because it didn't seem fair that she should have to suffer and he didn't.

During the workshop she had plenty of opportunity to vent her anger, knowing that she had the support of other participants who had been through similar experiences and could easily empathize with her. This helped her to reach a level of acceptance about the abortion. But she longed to experience a similar healing in her relationship with Paul. Since the abortion, they had had very little sex, and now the relationship was suffering.

A week after the workshop, Kathi and Paul arrived at my home for a private counseling session. He appeared to be a soft, gentle, considerate man. I asked him to describe their problem from his point of view. He complained that Kathi no longer initiated lovemaking, and when they did make love, it felt stilted and unnatural.

When I asked her to describe the problem, she said that whenever he was affectionate, he would then want to make love. She was so afraid of getting pregnant that this made her apprehensive of any kind of intimacy. And then, when they did make love, it caused an irritation in her genital area.

I asked them to lie side-by-side on the double bed, holding hands. I sat in an armchair beside them. I took them through a series of deep relaxation exercises, and the following session took place. The session was taped and this is a transcript which was made almost verbatim.

Joy: I want you both to imagine Kathi's uterus as a temple. See yourself standing in front of the temple, and observe it carefully. (I pause for a minute.) Now Paul, could you describe what you're seeing?

Paul: I see a pyramid. And it's very beautiful. But some of the pieces have crumbled off of it and have fallen onto the ground.

Joy: How does that feel to you, Kathi?

Kathi: Well, a pyramid feels dead, in a way. It's not really alive. It's got a big shell around it. But if it was smoothed out — if you could give it a lot of healing. . . I feel like your hands are healing, Paul. I know they are. I know they can be. So it feels like if you touched it and smoothed it and healed it, it would become more pink and rounded and healthy—the way it really looks.

Paul: Yes, I want to smooth it out. I feel that I want to use my hands.

Joy: Just see yourself doing that, Paul.

Paul: As I smooth it out, I sort of feel like I want to take the edges off. It's too abrasive. I want to make it a nicer shape. (Pause.) My hand and my stomach and my other hand holding Kathi's — they feel really big. They're huge. They feel so huge, it's funny.

Kathi: Do they feel healing big, or awkward big?

Paul: No, they feel healing big. I feel hot where my hand is and hot where my hand is holding you.

Joy: How would it feel to actually put your hands over Kathi's uterus? Do you want to do that, Paul?

Paul: Uh–huh.(He does.)

Joy: (Pause.) I feel a lot of love between you. That wounding that has happened around your sexuality is something that you don't need to hold onto. You need to be cautious, but you don't need all the sharp edges. It's good to let it soften. To feel the warmth coming back. Feel the pinkness, feel the love.

I want you to see yourselves inside the Temple. Imagine that you've brought lots of beautiful colored flowers. Flowers with all their female genitalia intact. Then put the flowers around the temple. Feel the temple restored. There's a good vibration in the temple now. There's a lot of love. And the energy is flowing in a positive, loving way. You know that this is a sacred place. It's also a friendly place.

I'd like you to imagine the two of you in the temple. See yourself facing each other. And holding hands. I'd like you to feel the spirit of the baby. Just feel that spirit between you. Because your relationship, and your love for one another, did create another spirit. And that's a positive thing: it's a beautiful thing. So in some sense, you've made a child together—that's still there. It's perfectly okay. I'd like you to be able to embrace that child—to really love it, to open your hearts to it. Because if you reject the spirit of that child, then you're rejecting the spirit of the relationship.

You are not obliged to bring it into flesh—that's a whole other thing. Maybe ten years from now, you'll want to do that, but that's not required. But it's important to open your hearts to the spirit of the creative offspring of your relationship. How does that feel to you, Paul?

Paul: I've always treated the child as something that was really there, even though it wasn't in flesh.

Kathi: It feels really strong for me, too.

Joy: Okay, now, feel that spirit moving upward. Feel it going up into its own realm, where it's perfectly happy to be. Imagine moving closer to one another, so that you're embracing one another. Imagine that you're naked, and feel your flesh touching flesh, and feel the healing happening. Forgiveness. And the healing. And the gentleness. And the trust—coming back. And the promise to be more careful in the future.

See yourselves surrounded by white light. And that light is healing the relationship. Healing the sexual feelings. (Long pause.) Is there anything else that either one of you would like to do before you leave the temple?

Kathi: I'd just like to know that we're always going to feel its spirituality, and its potentiality, and not deny or hate its ability to create another spirit. To know that if ever it does again, even if we do have another abortion, that we really treasure that life.

Joy: Yes. How does that feel to you, Paul?

Paul: It's important that I have to respect that, and acknowledge that it was a spirit.

Kathi: And Paul, I'd like you to know that your entering my vagina is sort of like approaching the spirituality of my uterus, and to have the awareness that that potentiality to create another spirit is there every time that happens. So, when we do have intercourse, it's really special because of that, and it's really emotional because of that. I'd like to be able to keep that awareness, and to have intercourse only when it feels right that way. Because otherwise, I feel as if it's desecrating the temple.

Joy: How do you feel about that, Paul?

Paul: (Very long silence.) I see it. I'm just getting more of an understanding of the spiritual aspect of the uterus. I'm just beginning to grasp what it means—how much it means.

Kathi: Do you think it feels right for us to be able to do that?

Paul: It gives more meaning toward your uterus—rather than just a pleasurable sort of experience. Now that I see it in that light it makes just the sexual experience seem selfish or—insignificant. I feel warm toward your uterus now. It feels as if I'm closer to it. (Cries.) I feel that I've abused it.

Joy: Perhaps you two would like to hold each other. (They do.)

Paul: I've said I'm sorry to you, but I've never said I'm sorry to your uterus. (They both cry.)

Conclusion

Epilogue

How difficult it is to speak to you when I know nothing about your circumstances. I don't know whether this potential being is someone you would cherish, or if it is only a terrible inconvenience.

Life is precious. Conception is magic. Children can be such a blessing—if they're wanted.

I believe in God. And I believe this God loves us, and understands our grief and turmoil. Laws (like the Ten Commandments) are intended as guidelines. But wise judges are needed to interpret these laws. Abortion will always be an area of controversy because it is on that fine edge between life and death.

I believe that each case is unique, and each woman or couple who moves through this crisis should have access to someone who is sensitive, compassionate, and non-judgmental, who can help them to arrive at a decision that they can live with.

Please, be gentle with yourself. Don't judge yourself too harshly. If you believe you will be judged, then imagine this judge as someone who is kind and compassionate, someone who cares about you as a real person with real feelings. Because you are.

Appendix A
Bach Flower Remedies

Dr. Edward Bach had a successful private practice in London, England, in the early 1900's. He was a sensitive, caring man who became discouraged with traditional medicine. He saw that patients became ill when they were unhappy or emotionally off-balance and he believed that if he could find a way of healing their emotions, the physical problems would follow suit.

So Bach gave up his practice and moved to the countryside to pursue his vision. He found he could induce particular mental states in himself, and then he would look for the proper cure. And he found it—in the flowers.

He discovered that the flowers possess the power to alter our emotions. We all know how a favorite flower can make us smile when we're sad, or forgive when we're angry. Husbands often make intuitive use of this knowledge! The colors and odors and sheer beauty of flowers have the ability to influence and transform us in subtle ways.

Psychics have long known that the human body is surrounded by an aura (an energy field) of many colors. And when the emotions are disturbed, or when there is an illness within the body, the aura will reflect these problems. I believe that the flowers contain the essence of color, and that their subtle influence actually heals our auras. It has been shown by Kirlian photography (which captures energy patterns) that illness can be seen in the aura before it can be detected in the body. And thus, by healing the aura, it becomes possible to prevent or eliminate physical illness.

Dr. Bach devised a method for making special remedies from 38 different flowers, for various states of mind, and these are known as the Bach Flower Remedies. But his most popular contribution is a combination of five of these flowers, known as the Rescue Remedy. The emotions which these flowers influence will be quite familiar to most women (and some men) who find themselves unexpectedly pregnant:

Star of Bethlehem—for shock
Rock Rose—for terror and panic
Impatiens—for mental stress and tension
Cherry Plum—for desperation
Clematis—for a faint, faraway kind of feeling

Rescue Remedy is available in most herb stores and some health food stores. Or it may be ordered from Ellon Bach, USA, Inc., P.O. Box 320, Woodmere, New York 11598 or from the Edward Bach Centre in Mount Vernon, Sotwell, Wallingford, Berks., OX10 0PZ, England. They carry the full line of Bach Flower Remedies. Both places also carry Bach's books, *Heal Thyself* and *The Twelve Healers*.

Appendix B
Notes About Abortant Herbs

This book does not give specific abortants because too often women will use such remedies before carefully considering their choices. Then, if the remedy doesn't work, they may decide to keep the baby.

So far, no significant research has been done on the effects of abortants on the development of the fetus. This would be a worthwhile avenue of research. But until that time, I prefer to encourage the use of early pregnancy tests, good counseling, a thoughtful decision, and—when appropriate—an early vacuum abortion.

However, I must caution on the use of abortants because too many misinformed women have done harm to themselves. While some herbal and other abortants appear to be quite safe, some are very dangerous, particularly when taken in very large doses.

PENNYROYAL OIL (*Pulegium*) is a volatile oil related to turpentine, which works by irritating the kidneys and bladder and this in turn excites uterine contractions. The usual dose is .6 to 1.2 ml., but doses of 4 ml. have produced convulsions. In Colorado, 2 pregnant women took 1/4 oz. (about 7.5 ml.) of pennyroyal oil and were admitted to a hospital emergency room with symptoms of nausea, dizziness, and numbness of fingers. The symptoms went away by themselves for one woman, and overnight for the other woman. A third woman was brought to a hospital with severe abdominal pain and was vomiting blood. She then developed a skin rash and liver failure, and she died a week later. Two other cases of fetal poisoning with massive doses of pennyroyal oil have also been documented.

PENNYROYAL HERB is much milder than pennyroyal oil. The fresh European pennyroyal yields only about 1% pulegium and the stronger American variety yields about 2%. Pennyroyal tea made from either variety has not proven dangerous when taken in moderation (up to 5 cups per day for 5 days), but it has caused liver damage when taken in massive doses.

TANSY is an abortant herb which should be used with great caution, because it has been known to cause hemorrhaging in women who are prone to hemorrhage. In fact, tansy was used in large doses by American Indians who wished to commit suicide.

COTTONWOOD and MISTLETOE act directly upon the fetus, and *must not* be used if you have any thought of keeping the baby.

Appendix C
Shopping List

After reading this book, you may want to go to the store and buy some of the things I've described. To make this task easier, I've made a list of all the remedies mentioned. You can decide which ones are most appropriate for your situation, and check off the ones you think you might need.

To deal with stress (see page 31)

    Rescue Remedy—1 oz.

    Peppermint leaves—½ oz.

    Catnip leaves—½ oz.

    Scullcap leaves—½ oz.

    Calcium with Magnesium (see page 31)

    Vitamin B (see page 31)

    ascorbic acid tablets or powder or crystals

Preparing for an abortion (see page 60)

    Vitamin A—25,000 Unit perles

    Vitamin C with bioflavanoids in natural form, 250-500 mg.

    Vitamin E—400 I.U. perles

    Comfrey leaves—½ oz.

    Yarrow leaves—½ oz.

    Peppermint leaves—½ oz.

To diminish pain (see page 62)

    Rescue Remedy—1 oz. (this will be plenty to meet all your needs)

    Calcium or Calcium Magnesium

Follow-up after an abortion (see page 76)

    Vitamin B (as described on page 31,76)

    Comfrey leaves—1oz.

    Valerian root—1 oz.

    Yarrow—1 oz.

    Dong Quai (also spelled Tang Kuei)—the whole dried root is best; 2 or 3 roots. Or 5 Tbsp.

powdered root. Or about 50 tablets.

In case of heavy continuous bleeding (see page 80) choose one of the these:

(see page 80)

1) Angelica (any species should work)— 2 Tbsp. of root, or 1 Tbsp. of root powder with 12 00-size gelatin capsules, or a small amount of tincture, to use as directed on the bottle.

2) Shepherd's purse tea—4 tsp.

3) Cayenne—1 Tbsp. powder and 12 00-size capsules.

References

Boston Women's Health Book Collective, THE NEW OUR BODIES, OURSELVES—A Book by and for Women, (New York: Simon and Schuster, 1984).

CARAL Newsletter, February 26, 1986. Canadian Abortion Rights Action League.

Daniel Chu, "Choice vs. Life," *People*, August 5, 1985.

Margaret Doris, "The New Face of Adoption." *New Age Journal*. April, 1985.

M. Grieve, A MODERN HERBAL (New York: Dover Publications, 1971).

David Grimes, M.D., "Poisonings from an Herbal Abortifacient," *National Abortion Federation Quarterly*, Spring 1975.

Health Organizing Collective of New York Women's Health and Abortion Project, "Vacuum Aspiration Abortion" (pamphlet, 1971).

Martindale, THE EXTRA PHARMACOPOEIA, 26th edition, edited by Norman W. Blacow (London: The Pharmaceutical Press, 1972).

Linda McQuig et al., "The Nation's New Agony Over Abortion."*Maclean's*. July 25, 1983.

Lennart Nilsson, A CHILD IS BORN (New York: Delacorte Press, 1977).

O. Carl Simonton, M.D. and Stephanie Mattews-Simonton, GETTING WELL AGAIN (Toronto and New York: Bantam Books, 1981).

Sharon Smith, letter in *Mothering Magazine*, Fall 1984.

Lewis Vaughn, "Folk Remedies That Can Hurt You." *Prevention*. Vol. 36, No. 3. March, 1984.